BTEC National
Sport

Study Guide

A PEARSON COMPANY

BTEC National Study Guide: Sport

Published by:
Edexcel Limited
One90 High Holborn
London WC1V 7BH
www.edexcel.org.uk

Distributed by:
Pearson Education Limited
Edinburgh Gate
Harlow
Essex CM20 2JE

First published 2007

ISBN 978-1-84690-223-9

Project managed and typeset by Hart McLeod, Cambridge
Printed in Great Britain by Henry Ling Ltd., at the Dorset Press, Dorchester, Dorset

Cover image ©travelstock44/Alamy

The publisher's policy is to use paper manufactured from sustainable forests.

All reasonable efforts have been made to trace and contact original copyright owners.

This material offers high quality support for the delivery of Edexcel qualifications.
This does not mean that it is essential to achieve any Edexcel qualification, nor does it mean that this is the only suitable material available to support any Edexcel qualification. No Edexcel-published material will be used verbatim in setting any Edexcel assessment and any resource lists produced by Edexcel shall include this and other appropriate texts.

Acknowledgements

p.60 ©Blue Shadows/Alamy; p.101 ©John Rowley/Stone/Getty Images; p.115 ©Jim Cummins/Corbis; p.122 ©Dylan Martinez/Reuters/Corbis; p.132 brochure t ©Robert Michael/Corbis, c ©Aflo/Corbis, b ©Fred Mullane/NewSport/ Corbis; p.133 leaflet l ©Kieran Doherty/Reuters/Corbis, c ©Patrick Seeger/epa/Corbis, r ©Julian Smith/epa/Corbis; p.144 ©Hamish Blair/Staff/Getty Images; p.146 leaflet l ©Barbara Walton/epa/Corbis, r ©Randy Faris/Corbis; p.147 brochure l ©Paul Ellis/Staff/AFP/Getty Images r ©Ian Hodgson/Reuters/Corbis

Contents

If you've already followed a BTEC First programme, you will know that this is an exciting way to study; if you are fresh from GCSEs you will find that from now on you will be in charge of your own learning. This guide has been written specially for you, to help get you started and then succeed on your BTEC National course.

The **Introduction** concentrates on making sure you have all the right facts about your course at your fingertips. Also, it guides you through the important skills you need to develop if you want to do well including:

- managing your time
- researching information
- preparing a presentation.

Keep this by your side throughout your course and dip into it whenever you need to.

The **Activities** give you tasks to do on your own, in a small group or as a class. They will help you internalise your learning and then prepare for assessment by practising your skills and showing you how much you know. These activities are not for assessment.

The sample **Marked Assignments** show you what other students have done to gain Pass, Merit or Distinction. By seeing what past students have done, you should be able to improve your own grade.

Your BTEC National will cover six, twelve or eighteen units depending on whether you are doing an Award, Certificate or Diploma. In this guide the activities cover sections from Unit 1 – The Body in Action, Unit 2 – Health and Safety in Sport, Unit 4 – Sports Coaching and Unit 16 – Psychology for Sports Performance. These units underpin your study of Sport.

Because the guide covers only four units, it is essential that you do all the other work your tutors set you. You will have to research information in textbooks, in the library and on the Internet. You should have the opportunity to visit local organisations and welcome visiting speakers to your institution. This is a great way to find out more about your chosen vocational area – the type of jobs that are available and what the work is really like.

This guide is a taster, an introduction to your BTEC National. Use it as such and make the most of the rich learning environment that your tutors will provide for you. Your BTEC National will give you an excellent base for further study, a broad understanding of Sport and the knowledge you need to succeed in the world of work. Remember, thousands of students have achieved a BTEC National and are now studying for a degree or at work, building a successful career.

INTRODUCTION

SEVEN STEPS TO SUCCESS ON YOUR BTEC NATIONAL

You have received this guide because you have decided to do a BTEC National qualification. You may even have started your course. At this stage you should feel good about your decision. BTEC Nationals have many benefits – they are well-known and respected qualifications, they provide excellent preparation for future work or help you to get into university if that is your aim. If you are already at work then gaining a BTEC National will increase your value to your employer and help to prepare you for promotion.

Despite all these benefits though, you may be rather apprehensive about your ability to cope. Or you may be wildly enthusiastic about the whole course! More probably, you are somewhere between the two – perhaps quietly confident most of the time but sometimes worried that you may get out of your depth as the course progresses. You may be certain you made the right choice or still have days when your decision worries you. You may understand exactly what the course entails and what you have to do – or still feel rather bewildered, given all the new stuff you have to get your head around.

Your tutors will use the induction sessions at the start of your course to explain the important information they want you to know. At the time, though, it can be difficult to remember everything. This is especially true if you have just left school and are now studying in a new environment, among a group of people you have only just met. It is often only later that you think of useful questions to ask. Sometimes, misunderstandings or difficulties may only surface weeks or months into a course – and may continue for some time unless they are quickly resolved.

This student guide has been written to help to minimise these difficulties, so that you get the most out of your BTEC National course from day one. You can read through it at your own pace. You can look back at it whenever you have a problem or query.

This Introduction concentrates on making sure you have all the right facts about your course at your fingertips. This includes a **Glossary** (on page 32) which explains the specialist terms you may hear or read – including words and phrases highlighted in bold type in this Introduction.

The Introduction also guides you through the important skills you need to develop if you want to do well – such as managing your time, researching information and preparing a presentation; as well as reminding you about the key skills you will need to do justice to your work, such as good written and verbal communications.

Make sure you have all the right facts

- Use the PlusPoint boxes in each section to help you to stay focused on the essentials.

- Use the Action Point boxes to check out things you need to know or do right now.

- Refer to the Glossary (on page 32) if you need to check the meaning of any of the specialist terms you may hear or read.

Remember, thousands of students have achieved BTEC National Diplomas and are now studying for a degree or at work, building a successful career. Many were nervous and unsure of themselves at the outset – and very few experienced absolutely no setbacks during the course. What they did have, though, was a belief in their own ability to do well if they concentrated on getting things right one step at a time. This Introduction enables you to do exactly the same!

STEP ONE

UNDERSTAND YOUR COURSE AND HOW IT WORKS

What is a BTEC qualification and what does it involve? What will you be expected to do on the course? What can you do afterwards? How does this National differ from 'A' levels or a BTEC First qualification?

All these are common questions – but not all prospective students ask them! Did you? And, if so, did you really listen to the answers? And can you remember them now?

If you have already completed a BTEC First course then you may know some of the answers – although you may not appreciate some of the differences between that course and your new one.

Let's start by checking out the basics.

- All BTEC National qualifications are **vocational** or **work-related**. This doesn't mean that they give you all the skills that you need to do a job. It does mean that you gain the specific knowledge and understanding relevant to your chosen subject or area of work. This means that when you start in a job you will learn how to do the work more quickly and should progress further. If you are already employed, it means you become more valuable to your employer. You can choose to study a BTEC National in a wide range of vocational areas, such as Business, Health and Social Care, IT, Performing Arts and many others.

- There are three types of BTEC National qualification and each has a different number of units.

  - The BTEC National Award usually has 6 units and takes 360 **guided learning hours (GLH)** to complete. It is often offered as a part-time or short course but you may be one of the many students doing an Award alongside A-levels as a full-time course. An Award is equivalent to one 'A' level.

  - The BTEC National Certificate usually has 12 units and takes 720 GLH to complete. You may be able to study for the Certificate on a part-time or full-time course. It is equivalent to two 'A' levels.

– The BTEC National Diploma usually has 18 units and takes 1080 GLH to complete. It is normally offered as a two-year full-time course. It is equivalent to three 'A' levels.

These qualifications are often described as **nested**. This means that they fit inside each other (rather like Russian dolls!) because the same units are common to them all. This means that if you want to progress from one to another you can do so easily by simply completing more units.

- Every BTEC National qualification has a set number of **core units**. These are the compulsory units every student must complete. The number of core units you will do on your course depends upon the vocational area you are studying.

- All BTEC National qualifications also have a range of **specialist units** from which you may be able to make a choice. These enable you to study particular areas in more depth.

- Some BTEC National qualifications have **specialist core units**. These are mandatory units you will have to complete if you want to follow a particular pathway in certain vocational areas. Engineering is an example of a qualification with the over-arching title, Engineering, which has a set of core units that all students must complete. Then, depending what type of engineering a student wants to follow, there are more specialist core units that must be studied.

- On all BTEC courses you are expected to be in charge of your own learning. If you have completed a BTEC First, you will already have been introduced to this idea, but you can expect the situation to be rather different now that you are working at BTEC National level. Students on a BTEC First course will be expected to need more guidance whilst they develop their skills and find their feet. In some cases, this might last quite some time. On a BTEC National course you will be expected to take more responsibility for yourself and your own learning almost from the outset. You will quickly be expected to start thinking for yourself. This means planning what to do and carrying out a task without needing constant reminders. This doesn't mean that your tutor won't give you help and guidance when you need it. It does mean, though, that you need to be 'self-starting' and to be able to use your own initiative. You also need to be able to assess your own performance and make improvements when necessary. If you enjoy having the freedom to make your own decisions and work at your own pace then you will welcome this type of learning with open arms. However, there are dangers! If you are a procrastinator (look up this word if you don't know what it means!) then it's quite likely you will quickly get in a muddle. In this case read Step 3 – Use your time wisely – very carefully indeed!

- The way you are assessed and graded on a BTEC course is different from an 'A' level course, although you will still obtain UCAS points which you need if you want to go to university. You can read about this in the next section.

PLUSPOINTS

+ You can usually choose to study part-time or full-time for your BTEC National and do an Award, Certificate or Diploma and progress easily from one to the other.

+ You will study both core units and specialist units on your course.

+ When you have completed your BTEC course you can get a job (or **apprenticeship**), use your qualification to develop your career and/or continue your studies to degree level.

+ You are responsible for your own learning on a BTEC course. This prepares you for life at work or at university when you will be expected to be self-starting and to use your own initiative.

ACTION POINTS

✓ Check you know whether you are studying for an Award, Certificate or Diploma and find out the number of units you will be studying for your BTEC National qualification.

✓ Find out which are core and which are specialist units, and which specialist units are offered at your school or college.

✓ Check out the length of your course and when you will be studying each unit.

✓ Explore the Edexcel website at www.edexcel.org.uk. Your first task is to find what's available for your particular BTEC National qualification. Start by finding National qualifications, then look for your vocational area and check you are looking at the 2007 schemes. Then find the specification for your course. Don't print this out – it is far too long. You could, of course, save it if you want to refer to it regularly or you could just look through it for interest and then bookmark the pages relating to your qualification for future reference.

✓ Score yourself out of 5 (where 0 is awful and 5 is excellent) on each of the following to see how much improvement is needed for you to become responsible for your own learning!

Being punctual; organisational ability; tidiness; working accurately; finding and correcting own mistakes; solving problems; accepting responsibility; working with details; planning how to do a job; using own initiative; thinking up new ideas; meeting deadlines.

✓ Draw up your own action plan to improve any areas where you are weak. Talk this through at your next individual **tutorial**.

STEP TWO

UNDERSTAND HOW YOU ARE ASSESSED AND GRADED – AND USE THIS KNOWLEDGE TO YOUR ADVANTAGE!

If you already have a BTEC First qualification, you may think that you don't need to read this section because you assume that BTEC National is simply more of the same. Whilst there are some broad similarities, you will now be working at an entirely different level and the grades you get for your work could be absolutely crucial to your future plans.

Equally, if you have opted for BTEC National rather than 'A' level because you thought you would have less work (or writing) to do then you need to read this section very carefully. Indeed, if you chose your BTEC National because you thought it would guarantee you an easy life, you are likely to get quite a shock when reality hits home!

It is true that, unlike 'A' levels, there are no exams on a BTEC course. However, to do well you need to understand the importance of your assignments, how these are graded and how these convert into unit points and UCAS points. This is the focus of this section.

Your assignments

On a BTEC National course your learning is assessed by means of **assignments** set by your tutors and given to you to complete throughout your course.

■ Your tutors will use a variety of **assessment methods**, such as case studies, projects, presentations and shows to obtain evidence of your skills and knowledge to date. You may also be given work-based or **time-constrained** assignments – where your performance might be observed and assessed. It will depend very much on the vocational area you are studying (see also page 16).

- Important skills you will need to learn are how to research information (see page 25) and how to use your time effectively, particularly if you have to cope with several assignments at the same time (see page 12). You may also be expected to work cooperatively as a member of a team to complete some parts of your assignments – especially if you are doing a subject like Performing Arts – or to prepare a presentation (see page 26).

- All your assignments are based on **learning outcomes** set by Edexcel. These are listed for each unit in your course specification. You have to meet *all* the learning outcomes to pass the unit.

Your grades

On a BTEC National course, assignments that meet the learning outcomes are graded as Pass, Merit or Distinction.

- The difference between these grades has very little to do with how much you write! Edexcel sets out the **grading criteria** for the different grades in a **grading grid**. This identifies the **higher-level skills** you have to demonstrate to earn a higher grade. You can find out more about this, and read examples of good (and not so good) answers to assignments at Pass, Merit and Distinction level in the marked assignments section starting on page 125. You will also find out more about getting the best grade you can in Step 5 – Understand your assessment – on page 16.

- Your grades for all your assignments earn you **unit points**. The number of points you get for each unit is added together and your total score determines your final grade(s) for the qualification – again either Pass, Merit or Distinction. You get one final grade if you are taking a BTEC National Award, two if you are taking a BTEC National Certificate and three if you are taking a BTEC National Diploma.

- Your points and overall grade(s) also convert to **UCAS points** which you will need if you want to apply to study on a degree course. As an example, if you are studying a BTEC National Diploma, and achieve three final pass grades you will achieve 120 UCAS points. If you achieve three final distinction grades the number of UCAS points you have earned goes up to 360.

- It is important to note that you start earning both unit and UCAS points from the very first assignment you complete! This means that if you take a long time to settle into your course, or to start working productively, you could easily lose valuable points for quite some time. If you have your heart set on a particular university or degree course then this could limit your choices. Whichever way you look at it, it is silly to squander potentially good grades for an assignment and their equivalent points, just because you didn't really understand what you had to do – which is why this guide has been written to help you!

- If you take a little time to understand how **grade boundaries** work, you can see where you need to concentrate your efforts to get the best final grade possible. Let's give a simple example. Chris and Shaheeda both want to go to university and have worked hard on their BTEC National Diploma course. Chris ends with a total score of 226 unit points which converts to 280 UCAS points. Shaheeda ends with a total score of 228 unit points – just two points more – which converts to 320 UCAS points! This is because a score of between 204 and 227 unit points gives 280 UCAS points, whereas a score of 228 – 251 points gives 320 UCAS points. Shaheeda is pleased because this increases her chances of getting a place on the degree course she wants. Chris is annoyed. He says if he had known then he would have put more effort into his last assignment to get two points more.

■ It is always tempting to spend time on work you like doing, rather than work you don't – but this can be a mistake if you have already done the best you can at an assignment and it would already earn a very good grade. Instead you should now concentrate on improving an assignment which covers an area where you know you are weak, because this will boost your overall grade(s). You will learn more about this in Step 3 – Use your time wisely.

PLUSPOINTS

+ Your learning is assessed in a variety of ways, such as by assignments, projects and case studies. You will need to be able to research effectively, manage your own time and work well with other people to succeed.

+ You need to demonstrate specific knowledge and skills to achieve the learning outcomes set by Edexcel. You need to demonstrate you can meet all the learning outcomes to pass a unit.

+ Higher-level skills are required for higher grades. The grading criteria for Pass, Merit and Distinction grades are set out in a grading grid for the unit.

+ The assessment grades of Pass, Merit and Distinction convert to unit points. The total number of unit points you receive during the course determines your final overall grade(s) and the UCAS points you have earned.

+ Working effectively from the beginning maximises your chances of achieving a good qualification grade. Understanding grade boundaries enables you to get the best final grade(s) possible.

ACTION POINTS

✓ Find the learning outcomes for the units you are currently studying. Your tutor may have given you these already, or you can find them in the specification for your course that you already accessed at www.edexcel.org.uk.

✓ Look at the grading grid for the units and identify the way the evidence required changes to achieve the higher grades. Don't worry if there are some words that you do not understand – these are explained in more detail on page 32 of this guide.

✓ If you are still unsure how the unit points system works, ask your tutor to explain it to you.

✓ Check out the number of UCAS points you would need for any course or university in which you are interested.

✓ Keep a record of the unit points you earn throughout your course and check regularly how this is affecting your overall grade(s), based on the grade boundaries for your qualification. Your tutor will give you this information or you can check it yourself in the specification for your course on the Edexcel website.

STEP THREE

USE YOUR TIME WISELY

Most students on a BTEC National course are trying to combine their course commitments with a number of others – such as a job (either full or part-time) and family responsibilities. In addition, they still want time to meet with friends, enjoy a social life and keep up hobbies and interests that they have.

Starting the course doesn't mean that you have to hide away for months if you want to do well. It does mean that you have to use your time wisely if you want to do well, stay sane and keep a balance in your life.

You will only do this if you make time work for you, rather than against you, by taking control. This means that you decide what you are doing, when you are doing it and work purposefully; rather than simply reacting to problems or panicking madly because you've yet another deadline staring you in the face.

This becomes even more important as your course progresses because your workload is likely to increase, particularly towards the end of a term. In the early days you may be beautifully organised and able to cope easily. Then you may find you have several tasks to complete simultaneously as well as some research to start. Then you get two assignments in the same week from different tutors – as well as having a presentation to prepare. Then another assignment is scheduled for the following week – and so on. This is not because your tutors are being deliberately difficult. Indeed, most will try to schedule your assignments to avoid such clashes. The problem, of course, is that none of your tutors can assess your abilities until you have learned something – so if several units start and end at the same time it is highly likely there will be some overlap between your assignments.

To cope when the going gets tough, without collapsing into an exhausted heap, you need to learn a few time management skills.

- **Pinpoint where your time goes at the moment** Time is like money – it's usually difficult to work out where it all went! Work out how much time you currently spend at college, at work, at home and on social activities. Check, too, how much time you waste each week – and why this happens. Are you disorganised or do you easily get distracted? Then identify commitments that are vital and those that are optional so that you know where you can find time if you need to.

- **Plan when and where to work** It is unrealistic not to expect to do quite a lot of work for your course in your own time. It is also better to work regularly, and in relatively short bursts, than to work just once or twice a week for very long stretches. In addition to deciding when to work, and for how long, you also need to think about when and where to work. If you are a lark, you will work better early in the day; if you are an owl, you will be at your best later on. Whatever time you work, you need somewhere quiet so that you can concentrate and with space for books and other resources you need. If the words 'quiet oasis' and 'your house' are totally incompatible at any time of the day or night

Use your time wisely

11

then check out the opening hours of your local and college library so that you have an escape route if you need it. If you are trying to combine studying with parental responsibilities it is sensible to factor in your children's commitments – and work around their bedtimes too! Store up favours, too, from friends and grandparents that you can call in if you get desperate for extra time when an assignment deadline is looming.

- **Schedule your commitments** Keep a diary or (even better) a wall chart and write down every appointment you make or task you are given. It is useful to use a colour code to differentiate between personal and work or course commitments. You may also want to enter assignment review dates with your tutor in one colour and final deadline dates in another. Keep your diary or chart up-to-date by adding any new dates promptly every time you receive another task or assignment or whenever you make any other arrangements. Keep checking ahead so that you always have prior warning when important dates are looming. This stops you from planning a heavy social week when you will be at your busiest at work or college and from arranging a dental appointment on the morning when you and your team are scheduled to give an important presentation!

- **Prioritise your work** This means doing the most important and urgent task first, rather than the one you like the most! Normally this will be the task or assignment with the nearest deadline. There are two exceptions. Sometimes you may need to send off for information and allow time for it to arrive. It is therefore sensible to do this first so that you are not held up later. The second is when you have to take account of other people's schedules – because you are working in a team or are arranging to interview someone, for example. In this case you will have to arrange your schedule around their needs, not just your own.

- **Set sensible timescales** Trying to do work at the last minute or in a rush is never satisfactory, so it is wise always to allocate more time than you think you will need, never less. Remember, too, to include all the stages of a complex task or assignment, such as researching the information, deciding what to use, creating a first draft, checking it and making improvements and printing it out. If you are planning to do any of your work in a central facility always allow extra time and try to start work early. If you arrive at the last minute you may find every computer and printer is fully utilised until closing time.

- **Learn self-discipline!** This means not putting things off (procrastinating!) because you don't know where to start or don't feel in the mood. Unless you are ill, you have to find some way of persuading yourself to work. One way is to bribe yourself. Make a start and promise yourself that if you work productively for 30 minutes then you deserve a small reward. After 30 minutes you may have become more engrossed and want to keep going a little longer. Otherwise at least you have made a start, so it's easier to come back and do more later. It doesn't matter whether you have research to do, an assignment to write up, a coaching session to plan, or lines to learn, you need to be self-disciplined.

- **Take regular breaks and keep your life in balance** Don't go to the opposite extreme and work for hours on end. Take regular breaks to give yourself a rest and a change of activity. You need to recharge your batteries! Similarly, don't cancel every social arrangement so that you can work 24/7. Whilst this may be occasionally necessary if you have several deadlines looming simultaneously, it should only be a last resort. If you find yourself doing this regularly then go back to the beginning of this section and see where your time-management planning is going wrong.

PLUSPOINTS

+ Being in control of your time enables you to balance your commitments according to their importance and allows you not let to anyone down – including yourself.

+ Controlling time involves knowing how you spend (and waste!) your time now, planning when best to do work, scheduling your commitments and setting sensible timescales for work to be done.

+ Knowing how to prioritise means that you will schedule work effectively according to its urgency and importance but this also requires self-discipline. You have to follow the schedule you have set for yourself!

+ Managing time and focusing on the task at hand means you will do better work and be less stressed, because you are not having to react to problems or crises. You can also find the time to include regular breaks and leisure activities in your schedule.

ACTION POINTS

✓ Find out how many assignments you can expect to receive this term and when you can expect to receive these. Enter this information into your student diary or onto a planner you can refer to regularly.

✓ Update your diary and/or planner with other commitments that you have this term – both work/college-related and social. Identify any potential clashes and decide the best action to take to solve the problem.

✓ Identify your own best time and place to work quietly and effectively.

✓ Displacement activities are things we do to put off starting a job we don't want to do – such as sending texts, watching TV, checking emails etc. Identify yours so that you know when you're doing them!

STEP FOUR

UTILISE ALL YOUR RESOURCES

Your resources are all the things that can help you to achieve your qualification. They can therefore be as wide-ranging as your favourite website and your **study buddy** (see page 15) who collects handouts for you if you miss a class.

Your college will provide the essential resources for your course, such as a library with a wide range of books and electronic reference sources, learning resource centre(s), the computer network and Internet access. Other basic resources you will be expected to provide yourself, such as file folders and paper. The policy on textbooks varies from one college to another, but on most courses today students are expected to buy their own. If you look after yours carefully, then you have the option to sell it on to someone else afterwards and recoup some of your money. If you scribble all over it, leave it on the floor and then tread on it, turn back pages and rapidly turn it into a dog-eared, misshapen version of its former self then you miss out on this opportunity.

Unfortunately students often squander other opportunities to utilise resources in the best way – usually because they don't think about them very much, if at all. To help, below is a list of the resources you should consider important – with a few tips on how to get the best out of them.

- **Course information** This includes your course specification, this Study Guide and all the other information relating to your BTEC National which you can find on the Edexcel website. Add to this all the information given to you at college relating to your course, including term dates, assignment dates and, of course, your timetable. This should not be 'dead' information that you glance at once and then discard or ignore. Rather it is important reference material that you need to store somewhere obvious, so that you can look at it whenever you have a query or need to clarify something quickly.

- **Course materials** In this group is your textbook (if there is one), the handouts you are given as well as print-outs and notes you make yourself. File handouts the moment you are given them and put them into an A4 folder bought for the purpose. You will need one for each unit you study. Some students prefer lever-arch files but these are more bulky so more difficult to carry around all day. Unless you have a locker at college it can be easier to keep a lever arch file at home for permanent storage of past handouts and notes for a unit and carry an A4 folder with you which contains current topic information. Filing handouts and print-outs promptly means they don't get lost. They are also less likely to get crumpled, torn or tatty becoming virtually unreadable. Unless you have a private and extensive source of income then this is even more important if you have to pay for every print-out you take in your college resource centre. If you are following a course such as Art and Design, then there will be all your art materials and the pieces you produce. You must look after these with great care.

- **Other stationery items** Having your own pens, pencils, notepad, punch, stapler and sets of dividers is essential. Nothing irritates tutors more than watching one punch circulate around a group – except, perhaps, the student who trudges into class with nothing to write on or with. Your dividers should be clearly labelled to help you store and find notes, print-outs and handouts fast. Similarly, your notes should be clearly headed and dated. If you are writing notes up from your own research then you will have to include your source. Researching information is explained in Step 6 – Sharpen your skills.

- **Equipment and facilities** These include your college library and resource centres, the college computer network and other college equipment you can use, such as laptop computers, photocopiers and presentation equipment. Much of this may be freely available; others – such as using the photocopier in the college library or the printers in a resource centre – may cost you money. Many useful resources will be electronic, such as DVDs or electronic journals and databases. At home you may have your own computer with Internet access to count as a resource. Finally, include any specialist equipment and facilities available for your particular course that you use at college or have at home.

Utilise all your resources

14

All centralised college resources and facilities are invaluable if you know how to use them – but can be baffling when you don't. Your induction should have included how to use the library, resource centre(s) and computer network. You should also have been informed of the policy on using IT equipment which determines what you can and can't do when you are using college computers. If, by any chance, you missed this then go and check it out for yourself. Library and resource centre staff will be only too pleased to give you helpful advice – especially if you pick a quiet time to call in. You can also find out about the allowable ways to transfer data between your college computer and your home computer if your options are limited because of IT security.

Having a study buddy is a good idea

■ **People** You are surrounded by people who are valuable resources: your tutor(s), specialist staff at college, your employer and work colleagues, your relatives and any friends who have particular skills or who work in the same area you are studying. Other members of your class are also useful resources – although they may not always seem like it! Use them, for example, to discuss topics out of class time. A good debate between a group of students can often raise and clarify issues that there may not be time to discuss fully in class. Having a study buddy is another good idea – you get/make notes for them when they are away and vice versa. That way you don't miss anything.

If you want information or help from someone, especially anyone outside your immediate circle, then remember to get the basics right! Approach them courteously, do your homework first so that you are well-prepared and remember that you are asking for assistance – not trying to get them to do the work for you! If someone has agreed to allow you to interview them as part of your research for an assignment or project then good preparations will be vital, as you will see in Step 6 – Sharpen your Skills (see page 22).

One word of warning: be wary about using information from friends or relatives who have done a similar or earlier course. First, the slant of the material they were given may be different. It may also be out-of-date. And *never* copy anyone else's written assignments. This is **plagiarism** – a deadly sin in the educational world. You can read more about this in Step 5 – Understand your assessment (see page 16).

■ **You!** You have the ability to be your own best resource or your own worst enemy! The difference depends upon your work skills, your personal skills and your attitude to your course and other people. You have already seen how to use time wisely. Throughout this guide you will find out how to sharpen and improve other work and personal skills and how to get the most out of your course – but it is up to you to read it and apply your new-found knowledge! This is why attributes like a positive attitude, an enquiring mind and the ability to focus on what is important all have a major impact on your final result.

15

PLUSPOINTS

+ Resources help you to achieve your qualification. You will squander these unwittingly if you don't know what they are or how to use them properly.

+ Course information needs to be stored safely for future reference: course materials need to be filed promptly and accurately so that you can find them quickly.

+ You need your own set of key stationery items; you also need to know how to use any central facilities or resources such as the library, learning resource centres and your computer network.

+ People are often a key resource – school or college staff, work colleagues, members of your class, people who are experts in their field.

+ You can be your own best resource! Develop the skills you need to be able to work quickly and accurately and to get the most out of other people who can help you.

ACTION POINTS

✓ Under the same headings as in this section, list all the resources you need for your course and tick off those you currently have. Then decide how and when you can obtain anything vital that you lack.

✓ Check that you know how to access and use all the shared resources to which you have access at school or college.

✓ Pair up with someone on your course as a study buddy – and don't let them down!

✓ Test your own storage systems. How fast can you find notes or print-outs you made yesterday/last week/last month – and what condition are they in?

✓ Find out the IT policy at your school or college and make sure you abide by it.

16

STEP FIVE

UNDERSTAND YOUR ASSESSMENT

The key to doing really, really well on any BTEC National course is to understand exactly what you are expected to do in your assignments – and then to do it! It really is as simple as that. So why is it that some people go wrong?

Obviously you may worry that an assignment may be so difficult that it is beyond you. Actually this is highly unlikely to happen because all your assignments are based on topics you will have already covered thoroughly in class. Therefore, if you have attended regularly – and have clarified any queries or worries you have either in class or during your tutorials – this shouldn't happen. If you have had an unavoidable lengthy absence then you may need to review your progress with your tutor and decide how best to cope with the situation. Otherwise, you should note that the main problems with assignments are usually due to far more mundane pitfalls – such as:

✗ not reading the instructions or the assignment brief properly

✗ not understanding what you are supposed to do

✗ only doing part of the task or answering part of a question

✗ skimping the preparation, the research or the whole thing

✗ not communicating your ideas clearly

✗ guessing answers rather than researching properly

✗ padding out answers with irrelevant information

✗ leaving the work until the last minute and then doing it in a rush

✗ ignoring advice and feedback your tutor has given you.

You can avoid all of these traps by following the guidelines below so that you know exactly what you are doing, prepare well and produce your best work.

The assignment 'brief'

The word 'brief' is just another way of saying 'instructions'. Often, though, a 'brief' (despite its name!) may be rather longer. The brief sets the context for the work, defines what evidence you will need to produce and matches the grading criteria to the tasks. It will also give you a schedule for completing the tasks. For example, a brief may include details of a case study you have to read; research you have to carry out or a task you have to do, as well as questions you have to answer. Or it may give you details about a project or group presentation you have to prepare. The type of assignments you receive will depend partly upon the vocational area you are studying, but you can expect some to be in the form of written assignments. Others are likely to be more practical or project-based, especially if you are doing a very practical subject such as Art and Design, Performing Arts or Sport. You may also be assessed in the workplace. For example, this is a course requirement if you are studying Children's Care, Learning and Development.

The assignment brief may also include the **learning outcomes** to which it relates. These tell you the purpose of the assessment and the knowledge you need to demonstrate to obtain a required grade. If your brief doesn't list the learning outcomes, then you should check this information against the unit specification to see the exact knowledge you need to demonstrate.

The grade(s) you can obtain will also be stated on the assignment brief. Sometimes an assignment will focus on just one grade. Others may give you the opportunity to develop or extend your work to progress to a higher grade. This is often dependent upon submitting acceptable work at the previous grade first. You will see examples of this in the Marked Assignment section of this Study Guide starting on page 125.

The brief will also tell you if you have to do part of the work as a member of a group. In this case, you must identify your own contribution. You may also be expected to take part in a **peer review**, where you all give feedback on the contribution of one another. Remember that you should do this as objectively and professionally as possible – not just praise everyone madly in the hope that they will do the same for you! In any assignment where there is a group contribution, there is virtually always an individual component, so that your individual grade can be assessed accurately.

Finally, your assignment brief should state the final deadline for handing in the work as well as any interim review dates when you can discuss your progress and ideas with your tutor. These are very important dates indeed and should be entered immediately into your diary or planner. You should schedule your work around these dates so that you have made a start by the first date. This will then enable you to note any queries or significant issues you want to discuss. Otherwise you will waste a valuable opportunity to obtain useful feedback on your progress. Remember, too, to take a notebook to any review meetings so that you can write down the guidance you are given.

Your school or college rules and regulations

Your school or college will have a number of policies and guidelines about assignments and assessment. These will deal with issues such as:

- The procedure you must follow if you have a serious personal problem so cannot meet the deadline date and need an extension.
- Any penalties for missing a deadline date without any good reason.
- The penalties for copying someone else's work (**plagiarism**). These will be severe so make sure that you never share your work (including your CDs) with anyone else and don't ask to borrow theirs.
- The procedure to follow if you are unhappy with the final grade you receive.

Even though it is unlikely that you will ever need to use any of these policies, it is sensible to know they exist, and what they say, just as a safeguard.

Understanding the question or task

There are two aspects to a question or task that need attention. The first are the *command words*, which are explained below. The second are the *presentation instructions*, so that if you are asked to produce a table or graph or report then you do exactly that – and don't write a list or an essay instead!

Command words are used to specify how a question must be answered, eg 'explain', 'describe', 'analyse', 'evaluate'. These words relate to the type of answer required. So whereas you may be asked to 'describe' something at Pass level, you will need to do more (such as 'analyse' or 'evaluate') to achieve Merit or Distinction grade.

Many students fail to get a higher grade because they do not realise the difference between these words. They simply don't know *how* to analyse or evaluate, so give an explanation instead. Just adding to a list or giving a few more details will never give you a higher grade – instead you need to change your whole approach to the answer.

The **grading grid** for each unit of your course gives you the command words, so that you can find out exactly what you have to do in each unit, to obtain a Pass, Merit and Distinction. The following charts show you what is usually required when you see a particular command word. You can use this, and the marked assignments on pages 125–158, to see the difference between the types of answers required for each grade. (The assignments your centre gives you will be specially written to ensure you have the opportunity to achieve all the possible grades.) Remember, though, that these are just examples to guide you. The exact response will often depend upon the way a question is worded, so if you have any doubts at all check with your tutor before you start work.

There are two other important points to note:

- Sometimes the same command word may be repeated for different grades – such as 'create' or 'explain'. In this case the *complexity* or *range* of the task itself increases at the higher grades – as you will see if you read the grading grid for the unit.

- Command words can also vary depending upon your vocational area. If you are studying Performing Arts or Art and Design you will probably find several command words that an Engineer or IT Practitioner would not – and vice versa!

To obtain a Pass grade

To achieve this grade you must usually demonstrate that you understand the important facts relating to a topic and can state these clearly and concisely.

Command word	What this means
Create (or produce)	Make, invent or construct an item.
Describe	Give a clear, straightforward description that includes all the main points and links these together logically.
Define	Clearly explain what a particular term means and give an example, if appropriate, to show what you mean.
Explain . . . how/why	Set out in detail the meaning of something, with reasons. It is often helpful to give an example of what you mean. Start with the topic then give the 'how' or 'why'.
Identify	Distinguish and state the main features or basic facts relating to a topic.
Interpret	Define or explain the meaning of something.
Illustrate	Give examples to show what you mean.
List	Provide the information required in a list rather than in continuous writing.
Outline	Write a clear description that includes all the main points but avoid going into too much detail.
Plan (or devise)	Work out and explain how you would carry out a task or activity.
Select (and present) information	Identify relevant information to support the argument you are making and communicate this in an appropriate way.
State	Write a clear and full account.
Undertake	Carry out a specific activity.
Examples: **Identify** the main features on a digital camera. **Describe** your usual lifestyle. **Outline** the steps to take to carry out research for an assignment.	

To obtain a Merit grade

To obtain this grade you must prove that you can apply your knowledge in a specific way.

Command word	What this means
Analyse	Identify separate factors, say how they are related and how each one relates to the topic.
Classify	Sort your information into appropriate categories before presenting or explaining it.
Compare and contrast	Identify the main factors that apply in two or more situations and explain the similarities and differences or advantages and disadvantages.
Demonstrate	Provide several relevant examples or appropriate evidence which support the arguments you are making. In some vocational areas this may also mean giving a practical performance.
Discuss	Provide a thoughtful and logical argument to support the case you are making.
Explain (in detail)	Provide details and give reasons and/or evidence to clearly support the argument you are making.
Implement	Put into practice or operation. You may also have to interpret or justify the effect or result.
Interpret	Understand and explain an effect or result.
Justify	Give appropriate reasons to support your opinion or views and show how you arrived at these conclusions.
Relate/report	Give a full account of, with reasons.
Research	Carry out a full investigation.
Specify	Provide full details and descriptions of selected items or activities.
Examples:	

Examples:

Compare and contrast the performance of two different digital cameras.
Justify your usual lifestyle.
Explain in detail the steps to take to research an assignment.

To obtain a Distinction grade

To obtain this grade you must prove that you can make a reasoned judgement based on appropriate evidence.

Command word	What this means
Analyse	Identify the key factors, show how they are linked and explain the importance and relevance of each.
Assess	Give careful consideration to all the factors or events that apply and identify which are the most important and relevant with reasons for your views.
Comprehensively explain	Give a very detailed explanation that covers all the relevant points and give reasons for your views or actions.
Comment critically	Give your view after you have considered all the evidence, particularly the importance of both the relevant positive and negative aspects.
Evaluate	Review the information and then bring it together to form a conclusion. Give evidence to support each of your views or statements.
Evaluate critically	Review the information to decide the degree to which something is true, important or valuable. Then assess possible alternatives taking into account their strengths and weaknesses if they were applied instead. Then give a precise and detailed account to explain your opinion.
Summarise	Identify review the main, relevant factors and/or arguments so that these are explained in a clear and concise manner.
Examples: **Assess** ten features commonly found on a digital camera. **Evaluate critically** your usual lifestyle. **Analyse** your own ability to carry out effective research for an assignment.	

Responding positively

This is often the most important attribute of all! If you believe that assignments give you the opportunity to demonstrate what you know and how you can apply it *and* positively respond to the challenge by being determined to give it your best shot, then you will do far better than someone who is defeated before they start.

It obviously helps, too, if you are well organised and have confidence in your own abilities – which is what the next section is all about!

PLUSPOINTS

+ Many mistakes in assignments are through errors that can easily be avoided such as not reading the instructions properly or doing only part of the task that was set!

+ Always read the assignment brief very carefully indeed. Check that you understand exactly what you have to do and the learning outcomes you must demonstrate.

+ Make a note of the deadline for an assignment and any interim review dates on your planner. Schedule work around these dates so that you can make the most of reviews with your tutor.

+ Make sure you know about school or college policies relating to assessment, such as how to obtain an extension or query a final grade.

+ For every assignment, make sure you understand the command words, which tell you how to answer the question, and the presentation instructions, which say what you must produce.

+ Command words are shown in the grading grid for each unit of your qualification. Expect command words and/or the complexity of a task to be different at higher grades, because you have to demonstrate higher-level skills.

ACTION POINTS

✓ Discuss with your tutor the format (style) of assignments you are likely to receive on your course, eg assignments, projects, or practical work where you are observed.

✓ Check the format of the assignments in the Marked Assignments section of this book. Look at the type of work students did to gain a Pass and then look at the difference in the Merit answers. Read the tutor's comments carefully and ask your own tutor if there is anything you do not understand.

✓ Check out all the policies and guidelines at your school or college that relate to assessment and make sure you understand them.

✓ Check out the grading grid for the units you are currently studying and identify the command words for each grade. Then check you understand what they mean using the explanations above. If there are any words that are not included, ask your tutor to explain the meanings and what you would be required to do.

STEP SIX

SHARPEN YOUR SKILLS

To do your best in any assignment you need a number of skills. Some of these may be vocationally specific, or professional, skills that you are learning as part of your course – such as acting or dancing if you are taking a Performing Arts course or, perhaps, football if you are following a Sports course. Others, though, are broader skills that will help you to do well in assignments no matter what subjects or topics you are studying – such as communicating clearly and cooperating with others.

Some of these skills you will have already and in some areas you may be extremely proficient. Knowing where your weaknesses lie, though, and doing something about them has many benefits. You will work more quickly, more accurately *and* have increased confidence in your own abilities. As an extra bonus, all these skills also make you more effective at work – so there really is no excuse for not giving yourself a quick skills check and then remedying any problem areas.

This section contains hints and tips to help you check out and improve each of the following areas:

- Your numeracy skills
- Keyboarding and document preparation
- Your IT skills
- Your written communication skills
- Working with others
- Researching information
- Making a presentation
- Problem solving and staying focused

Improving your numeracy skills

Some people have the idea that they can ignore numeracy because this skill isn't relevant to their vocational area – such as Art and Design or Children's Care, Learning and Development. If this is how you think then you are wrong! Numeracy is a life skill that everyone needs, so if you can't carry out basic calculations accurately then you will have problems, often when you least expect them.

Fortunately there are several things you can do to remedy this situation:

- Practise basic calculations in your head and then check them on a calculator.
- Ask your tutor if there are any essential calculations which give you difficulties.
- Use your onscreen calculator (or a spreadsheet package) to do calculations for you when you are using your computer.
- Try your hand at Sudoku puzzles – either on paper or by using a software package or online at sites such as www.websudoku.com/.
- Investigate puzzle sites and brain training software, such as http://school.discovery.com/brainboosters/ and Dr Kawashima's Brain Training by Nintendo.
- Check out online sites such as www.bbc.co.uk/skillswise/ and www.bbc.co.uk/schools/ks3bitesize/maths/number/index.shtml to improve your skills.

Numeracy is a life skill

Keyboarding and document preparation

- Think seriously about learning to touch type to save hours of time! Your school or college may have a workshop you can join or you can learn online such as by downloading a free program at www.sense-lang.org/typing/ or practising on sites such as www.computerlab.kids.new.net/keyboarding.htm.
- Obtain correct examples of document formats you will have to use, such as a report or summary. Your tutor may provide you with these or you can find examples in many communication textbooks.
- Proof-read work you produce on a computer *carefully*. Remember that your spell checker will not pick up every mistake you make, such as a mistyped word that makes another word (eg form/from; sheer/shear)

23

and grammar checkers, too, are not without their problems! This means you still have to read your work through yourself. If possible, let your work go 'cold' before you do this so that you read it afresh and don't make assumptions about what you have written. Then read word by word to make sure it still makes sense and there are no silly mistakes, such as missing or duplicated words.

■ Make sure your work looks professional by using an appropriate typeface and font size as well as suitable margins.

■ Print out your work carefully and store it neatly, so it looks in pristine condition when you hand it in.

Your IT skills

■ Check that you can use the main features of all the software packages that you will need to produce your assignments, such as Word, Excel and PowerPoint.

■ Adopt a good search engine, such as Google, and learn to use it properly. Many have online tutorials such as www.googleguide.com.

■ Develop your IT skills to enable you to enhance your assignments appropriately. For example, this may include learning how to import and export text and artwork from one package to another; taking digital photographs and inserting them into your work and/or creating drawings or diagrams by using appropriate software for your course.

Your written communication skills

A poor vocabulary will reduce your ability to explain yourself clearly; work peppered with spelling or punctuation errors looks unprofessional.

■ Read more. This introduces you to new words and familiarises you over and over again with the correct way to spell words.

■ Look up words you don't understand in a dictionary and then try to use them yourself in conversation.

■ Use the Thesaurus in Word to find alternatives to words you find yourself regularly repeating, to add variety to your work.

■ *Never* use words you don't understand in the hope that they sound impressive!

■ Do crosswords to improve your word power and spelling.

■ Resolve to master punctuation – especially apostrophes – either by using an online programme or working your way through the relevant section of a communication textbook that you like.

■ Check out online sites such as www.bbc.co.uk/skillswise/ and www.bbc.co.uk/schools/gcsebitesize/english/ as well as puzzle sites with communication questions such as http://school.discovery.com/brainboosters/.

Working with others

In your private life you can choose who you want to be with and how you respond to them. At work you cannot do that – you are paid to be professional and this means working alongside a wide variety of people, some of whom you may like and some of whom you may not!

The same applies at school or college. By the time you have reached BTEC National level you will be expected to have outgrown wanting to work with your best friends on every project! You may not be very keen on everyone who is in the same team as you, but – at the very least – you can be pleasant, cooperative and helpful. In a large group this isn't normally too difficult. You may find it much harder if you have to partner someone who has very different ideas and ways of working to you.

In this case it may help if you:

- Realise that everyone is different and that your ways of working may not always be the best!
- Are prepared to listen and contribute to a discussion (positively) in equal amounts. Make sure, too, that you encourage the quiet members of the group to speak up by asking them what their views are. The ability to draw other people into the discussion is an important and valuable skill to learn.
- Write down what you have said you will do, so that you don't forget anything.
- Are prepared to do your fair share of the work.
- Discuss options and alternatives with people – don't give them orders or meekly accept instructions and then resent it afterwards.
- Don't expect other people to do what you wouldn't be prepared to do.
- Are sensitive to other people's feelings and remember that they may have personal problems or issues that affect their behaviour.
- *Always* keep your promises and never let anyone down when they are depending upon you.
- Don't flounce around or lose your temper if things get tough. Instead take a break while you cool down. Then sit down and discuss the issues that are annoying you.
- Help other people to reach a compromise when necessary, by acting as peacemaker.

Researching information

Poor researchers either cannot find what they want or find too much – and then drown in a pile of papers. If you find yourself drifting aimlessly around a library when you want information or printing out dozens of pages for no apparent purpose, then this section is for you!

- Always check *exactly* what it is you need to find and how much detail is needed. Write down a few key words to keep yourself focused.
- Discipline yourself to ignore anything that is irrelevant – from books with interesting titles to websites which sound tempting but have little to do with your topic or key words.
- Remember that you could theoretically research information forever! So at some time you have to call a halt. Learning when to do this is another skill, but you can learn this by writing out a schedule which clearly states when you have to stop looking and start sorting out your information and writing about it!

- In a library, check you know how the books are stored and what other types of media are available. If you can't find what you are looking for then ask the librarian for help. Checking the index in a book is the quickest way to find out whether it contains information related to your key words. Put it back if it doesn't or if you can't understand it. If you find three or four books and/or journals that contain what you need then that is usually enough.

- Online use a good search engine and use the summary of the search results to check out the best sites. Force yourself to check out sites beyond page one of the search results! When you enter a site investigate it carefully – use the site map if necessary. It isn't always easy to find exactly what you want. Bookmark sites you find helpful and will want to use again and only take print-outs when the information is closely related to your key words.

- Talk to people who can help you (see also Step 4 – Utilise all your resources) and prepare in advance by thinking about the best questions to ask. Always explain why you want the information and don't expect anyone to tell you anything that is confidential or sensitive – such as personal information or financial details. Always write clear notes so that you remember what you have been told, by whom and when. If you are wise you will also note down their contact details so that you can contact them again if you think of anything later. If you remember to be courteous and thank them for their help, this shouldn't be a problem.

- Store all your precious information carefully and neatly in a labelled folder so that you can find it easily. Then, when you are ready to start work, reread it and extract that which is most closely related to your key words and the task you are doing.

- Make sure you state the source of all the information you quote by including the name of the author or the web address, either in the text or as part of a bibliography at the end. Your school or college will have a help sheet which will tell you exactly how to do this.

Making a presentation

This involves several skills – which is why it is such a popular way of finding out what students can do! It will test your ability to work in a team, speak in public and use IT (normally PowerPoint) – as well as your nerves. It is therefore excellent practice for many of the tasks you will have to do when you are at work – from attending an interview to talking to an important client.

You will be less nervous if you have prepared well and have rehearsed your role beforehand. You will produce a better, more professional presentation if you take note of the following points.

- If you are working as a team, work out everyone's strengths and weaknesses and divide up the work (fairly) taking these into account. Work out, too, how long each person should speak and who would be the best as the 'leader' who introduces each person and then summarises everything at the end.

PLUSPOINTS

+ Poor numeracy skills can let you down in your assignments and at work. Work at improving these if you regularly struggle with even simple calculations.

+ Good keyboarding, document production and IT skills can save you hours of time and mean that your work is of a far more professional standard. Improve any of these areas which are letting you down.

+ Your written communication skills will be tested in many assignments. Work at improving areas of weakness, such as spelling, punctuation or vocabulary.

+ You will be expected to work cooperatively with other people both at work and during many assignments. Be sensitive to other people's feelings, not just your own, and always be prepared to do your fair share of the work and help other people when you can.

+ To research effectively you need to know exactly what you are trying to find and where to look. This means understanding how reference media is stored in your library as well as how to search online. Good organisation skills also help so that you store important information carefully and can find it later. And never forget to include your sources in a bibliography.

+ Making a presentation requires several skills and may be nerve-racking at first. You will reduce your problems if you prepare well, are not too ambitious and have several run-throughs beforehand. Remember to speak clearly and a little more slowly than normal and smile from time to time!

ACTION POINTS

✓ Test both your numeracy and literacy skills at http://www.move-on.org.uk/testyourskills.asp# to check your current level. You don't need to register on the site if you click to do the 'mini-test' instead. If either need improvement, get help at http://www.bbc.co.uk/keyskills/it/1.shtml.

✓ Do the following two tasks with a partner to jerk your brain into action!

 – Each write down 36 simple calculations in a list, eg 8 x 6, 19 – 8, 14 + 6. Then exchange lists. See who can answer the most correctly in the shortest time.

 – Each write down 30 short random words (no more than 8 letters), eg cave, table, happily. Exchange lists. You each have three minutes to try to remember as many words as possible. Then hand back the list and write down all those you can recall. See who can remember the most.

✓ Assess your own keyboarding, proof-reading, document production, written communication and IT skills. Then find out if your tutors agree with you!

✓ List ten traits in other people that drive you mad. Then, for each one, suggest what you could do to cope with the problem (or solve it) rather than make a fuss. Compare your ideas with other members of your group.

✓ Take a note of all feedback you receive from your tutors, especially in relation to working with other people, researching and giving presentations. In each case focus on their suggestions and ideas so that you continually improve your skills throughout the course.

27

- Don't be over-ambitious. Take account of your time-scale, resources and the skills of the team. Remember that a simple, clear presentation is often more professional than an over-elaborate or complicated one where half the visual aids don't work properly!

- If you are using PowerPoint try to avoid preparing every slide with bullet points! For variety, include some artwork and vary the designs. Remember that you should *never* just read your slides to the audience! Instead prepare notes that you can print out that will enable you to enhance and extend what the audience is reading.

- Your preparations should also include checking the venue and time; deciding what to wear and getting it ready; preparing, checking and printing any handouts; deciding what questions might be asked and how to answer these.

- Have several run-throughs beforehand and check your timings. Check, too, that you can be heard clearly. This means lifting up your head and 'speaking' to the back of the room a little more slowly and loudly than you normally do.

- On the day, arrive in plenty of time so that you aren't rushed or stressed. Remember that taking deep breaths helps to calm your nerves.

- Start by introducing yourself clearly and smile at the audience. If it helps, find a friendly face and pretend you are just talking to that person.

- Answer any questions honestly and don't exaggerate, guess or waffle. If you don't know the answer then say so!

- If you are giving the presentation in a team, help out someone else who is struggling with a question if you know the answer.

- Don't get annoyed or upset if you get any negative feedback afterwards. Instead take note so that you can concentrate on improving your own performance next time. And don't focus on one or two criticisms and ignore all the praise you received! Building on the good and minimising the bad is how everyone improves in life!

STEP SEVEN

MAXIMISE YOUR OPPORTUNITIES AND MANAGE YOUR PROBLEMS

Like most things in life, you may have a few ups and downs on your course – particularly if you are studying over quite a long time, such as one or two years. Sometimes everything will be marvellous – you are enjoying all the units, you are up-to-date with your work, you are finding the subjects interesting and having no problems with any of your research tasks. At other times you may struggle a little more. You may find one or two topics rather tedious, or there may be distractions or worries in your personal life that you have to cope with. You may struggle to concentrate on the work and do your best.

Rather than just suffering in silence or gritting your teeth if things go a bit awry it is sensible if you have an action plan to help you cope. Equally, rather than just accepting good opportunities for additional experiences or learning, it is also wise to plan how to make the best of these. This section will show you how to do this.

Making the most of your opportunities

The following are examples of opportunities to find out more about information relevant to your course or to try putting some of your skills into practice.

28

- **External visits** You may go out of college on visits to different places or organisations. These are not days off – there is a reason for making each trip. Prepare in advance by reading around relevant topics and make notes of useful information whilst you are there. Then write (or type) it up neatly as soon as you can and file it where you can find it again!

- **Visiting speakers** Again, people are asked to talk to your group for a purpose. You are likely to be asked to contribute towards questions that may be asked – which may be submitted in advance so that the speaker is clear on the topics you are studying. Think carefully about information that you would find helpful so that you can ask one or two relevant and useful questions. Take notes whilst the speaker is addressing your group, unless someone is recording the session. Be prepared to thank the speaker on behalf of your group if you are asked to do so.

- **Professional contacts** These will be the people you meet on work experience doing the real job that one day you hope to do. Make the most of meeting these people to find out about the vocational area of your choice.

- **Work experience** If you need to undertake practical work for any particular units of your BTEC National qualification, and if you are studying full-time, then your tutor will organise a work experience placement for you and talk to you about the evidence you need to obtain. You may also be issued with a special log book or diary in which to record your experiences. Before you start your placement, check that you are clear about all the details, such as the time you will start and leave, the name of your supervisor, what you should wear and what you should do if you are ill during the placement and cannot attend. Read and reread the units to which your evidence will apply and make sure you understand the grading criteria and what you need to obtain. Then make a note of appropriate headings to record your information. Try to make time to write up your notes, log book and/or diary every night, whilst your experiences are fresh in your mind.

- **In your own workplace** You may be studying your BTEC National qualification on a part-time basis and also have a full-time job in the same vocational area. Or you may be studying full-time and have a part-time job just to earn some money. In either case you should be alert to opportunities to find out more about topics that relate to your workplace, no matter how generally. For example, many BTEC courses include topics such as health and safety, teamwork, dealing with customers, IT security and communications – to name but a few. All these are topics that your employer will have had to address and finding out more about these will broaden your knowledge and help to give more depth to your assignment responses.

- **Television programmes, newspapers, Podcasts and other information sources.** No matter what vocational area you are studying, the media are likely to be an invaluable source of information. You should be alert to any news bulletins that relate to your studies as well as relevant information in more topical television programmes. For example, if you are studying Art and Design then you should make a particular effort to watch the *Culture Show* as well as programmes on artists, exhibitions or other topics of interest. Business students should find inspiration by watching *Dragons Den*, *The Apprentice* and the *Money Programme* and Travel and Tourism students should watch holiday, travel and adventure programmes. If you are studying Media, Music and Performing Arts then you are spoiled for choice! Whatever your vocational choice, there will be television and radio programmes of special interest to you.

Remember that you can record television programmes to watch later if you prefer, and check out newspaper headlines online and from sites such as BBC news. The same applies to Podcasts. Of course, to know which information is relevant means that you must be familiar with the content of all the units you are studying, so it is useful to know what topics you will be learning about in the months to come, as well as the ones you are covering now. That way you can recognise useful opportunities when they arise.

The media are invaluable sources of information

Minimising problems

If you are fortunate, any problems you experience on your course will only be minor ones. For example, you may struggle to keep yourself motivated every single day and there may be times that you are having difficulty with a topic. Or you may be struggling to work with someone else in your team or to understand a particular tutor.

During induction you should have been told which tutor to talk to in this situation, and who to see if that person is absent or if you would prefer to see someone else. If you are having difficulties which are distracting you and affecting your work then it is sensible to ask to see your tutor promptly so that you can talk in confidence, rather than just trusting to luck everything will go right again. It is a rare student who is madly enthusiastic about every part of a course and all the other people on the course, so your tutor won't be surprised and will be able to give you useful guidance to help you stay on track.

If you are very unlucky, you may have a more serious personal problem to deal with. In this case it is important that you know the main sources of help in your school or college and how to access these.

- **Professional counselling** There may be a professional counselling service if you have a concern that you don't want to discuss with any teaching staff. If you book an appointment to see a counsellor then you can be certain that nothing you say will ever be mentioned to another member of staff without your permission.

- **Student complaint procedures** If you have a serious complaint to make then the first step is to talk to a tutor, but you should be aware of the formal student complaint procedures that exist if you cannot resolve the problem informally. Note that these are only used for serious issues, not for minor difficulties.

- **Student appeals procedures** If you cannot agree with a tutor about a final grade for an assignment then you need to check the grading criteria and ask the tutor to explain how the grade was awarded. If you are still unhappy then you should see your personal tutor. If you still disagree then you have the right to make a formal appeal.

■ **Student disciplinary procedures** These exist so that all students who flout the rules in a school or college will be dealt with in the same way. Obviously it is wise to avoid getting into trouble at any time, but if you find yourself on the wrong side of the regulations do read the procedures carefully to see what could happen. Remember that being honest about what happened and making a swift apology is always the wisest course of action, rather than being devious or trying to blame someone else.

■ **Serious illness** Whether this affects you or a close family member, it could severely affect your attendance. The sooner you discuss the problem with your tutor the better. This is because you will be missing notes and information from the first day you do not attend. Many students under-estimate the ability of their tutors to find inventive solutions in this type of situation – from sending notes by post to updating you electronically if you are well enough to cope with the work.

PLUSPOINTS

+ Some students miss out on opportunities to learn more about relevant topics. This may be because they haven't read the unit specifications, so don't know what topics they will be learning about in future; haven't prepared in advance or don't take advantage of occasions when they can listen to an expert and perhaps ask questions. Examples of these occasions include external visits, visiting speakers, work experience, being at work and watching television.

+ Many students encounter minor difficulties, especially if their course lasts a year or two. It is important to talk to your tutor, or another appropriate person, promptly if you have a worry that is affecting your work.

+ All schools and colleges have procedures for dealing with important issues and problems such as serious complaints, major illnesses, student appeals and disciplinary matters. It is important to know what these are.

ACTION POINTS

✓ List the type of opportunities available on your course for obtaining more information and talking to experts. Then check with your tutor to make sure you haven't missed out any.

✓ Check out the content of each unit you will be studying so that you know the main topics you have still to study.

✓ Identify the type of information you can find on television, in newspapers and in Podcasts that will be relevant to your studies.

✓ Check out your school or college documents and procedures to make sure that you know who to talk to in a crisis and who you can see if the first person is absent.

✓ Find out where you can read a copy of the main procedures in your school or college that might affect you if you have a serious problem. Then do so.

AND FINALLY . . .

Don't expect this Introduction to be of much use if you skim through it quickly and then put it to one side. Instead, refer to it whenever you need to remind yourself about something related to your course.

The same applies to the rest of this Student Guide. The Activities in the next section have been written to help you to demonstrate your understanding of many of the key topics contained in the core or specialist units you are studying. Your tutor may tell you to do these at certain times; otherwise there is nothing to stop you working through them yourself!

Similarly, the Marked Assignments in the final section have been written to show you how your assignments may be worded. You can also see the type of response that will achieve a Pass, Merit and Distinction – as well as the type of response that won't! Read these carefully and if any comment or grade puzzles you, ask your tutor to explain it.

Then keep this guide in a safe place so that you can use it whenever you need to refresh your memory. That way, you will get the very best out of your course – and yourself!

GLOSSARY

Note: all words highlighted in bold in the text are defined in the glossary.

Accreditation of Prior Learning (APL)

APL is an assessment process that enables your previous achievements and experiences to count towards your qualification providing your evidence is authentic, current, relevant and sufficient.

Apprenticeships

Schemes that enable you to work and earn money at the same time as you gain further qualifications (an **NVQ** award and a technical certificate) and improve your key skills. Apprentices learn work-based skills relevant to their job role and their chosen industry. You can find out more at www.apprenticeships.org.uk/

Assessment methods

Methods, such as **assignments**, case studies and practical tasks, used to check that your work demonstrates the learning and understanding required for your qualification.

Assessor

The tutor who marks or assesses your work.

Assignment

A complex task or mini-project set to meet specific **grading criteria**.

Awarding body

The organisation which is responsible for devising, assessing and issuing qualifications. The awarding body for all BTEC qualifications is Edexcel.

Core units

On a BTEC National course these are the compulsory or mandatory units that all students must complete to gain the qualification. Some BTEC qualifications have an over-arching title, eg Engineering, but within Engineering you can choose different routes. In this case you will study both common core units that are common to all engineering qualifications and **specialist core unit(s)** which are specific to your chosen **pathway**.

Degrees

These are higher education qualifications which are offered by universities and colleges. Foundation degrees take two years to complete; honours degrees may take three years or longer. See also **Higher National Certificates and Diplomas**.

DfES

The Department for Education and Skills: this is the government department responsible for education issues. You can find out more at www.dfes.gov.uk

Distance learning

This enables you to learn and/or study for a qualification without attending an Edexcel centre although you would normally be supported by a member of staff who works there. You communicate with your tutor and/or the centre that organises the distance learning programme by post, telephone or electronically.

Educational Maintenance Award (EMA)

This is a means-tested award which provides eligible students under 19, who are studying a full-time course at school or college, with a cash sum of money every week. See http://www.dfes.gov.uk/financialhelp/ema/ for up-to-date details.

External verification

Formal checking by a representative of Edexcel of the way a BTEC course is delivered. This includes sampling various assessments to check content and grading.

Final major project

This is a major, individual piece of work that is designed to enable you to demonstrate you have achieved several learning outcomes for a BTEC National qualification in the creative or performing arts. Like all assessments, this is internally assessed.

Forbidden combinations

Qualifications or units that cannot be taken simultaneously because their content is too similar.

GLH

See **Guided Learning Hours** on page 34

Grade

The rating (Pass, Merit or Distinction) given to the mark you have obtained which identifies the standard you have achieved.

Grade boundaries

The pre-set points at which the total points you have earned for different units converts to the overall grade(s) for your qualification.

Grading criteria

The standard you have to demonstrate to obtain a particular grade in the unit, in other words, what you have to prove you can do.

Grading domains

The main areas of learning which support the **learning outcomes**.
On a BTEC National course these are: application of knowledge and
understanding; development of practical and technical skills; personal
development for occupational roles; application of generic and **key
skills**. Generic skills are basic skills needed wherever you work, such
as the ability to work cooperatively as a member of a team.

Grading grid

The table in each unit of your BTEC qualification specification that
sets out the **grading criteria**.

Guided Learning Hours (GLH)

The approximate time taken to deliver a unit which includes the
time taken for direct teaching, instruction and assessment and for
you to carry out directed assignments or directed individual study. It
does not include any time you spend on private study or researching
an assignment. The GLH determines the size of the unit. At BTEC
National level, units are either 30, 60, 90 or 120 guided learning
hours. By looking at the number of GLH a unit takes, you can see
the size of the unit and how long it is likely to take you to learn and
understand the topics it contains.

Higher education (HE)

Post-secondary and post-further education, usually provided by
universities and colleges.

Higher level skills

Skills such as evaluating or critically assessing complex information
that are more difficult than lower level skills such as writing a
description or making out a list. You must be able to demonstrate
higher level skills to achieve a Distinction grade.

Higher National Certificates and Diplomas

Higher National Certificates and Diplomas are vocational
qualifications offered at colleges around the country. Certificates
are part-time and designed to be studied by people who are already
in work; students can use their work experiences to build on their
learning. Diplomas are full-time courses – although often students
will spend a whole year on work experience part way through their
Diploma. Higher Nationals are roughly equivalent to half a degree.

Indicative reading

Recommended books and journals whose content is both suitable
and relevant for the unit.

Induction

A short programme of events at the start of a course designed to give
you essential information and introduce you to your fellow students and
tutors so that you can settle down as quickly and easily as possible.

Internal verification

The quality checks carried out by nominated tutor(s) at your school or college to ensure that all assignments are at the right level and cover appropriate learning outcomes. The checks also ensure that all **assessors** are marking work consistently and to the same standard.

Investors in People (IIP)

A national quality standard which sets a level of good practice for the training and development of people. Organisations must demonstrate their commitment to achieve the standard.

Key skills

The transferable, essential skills you need both at work and to run your own life successfully. They are: literacy, numeracy, IT, problem solving, working with others and self-management.

Learning outcomes

The knowledge and skills you must demonstrate to show that you have effectively learned a unit.

Learning support

Additional help that is available to all students in a school or college who have learning difficulties or other special needs. These include reasonable adjustments to help to reduce the effect of a disability or difficulty that would place a student at a substantial disadvantage in an assessment situation.

Levels of study

The depth, breadth and complexity of knowledge, understanding and skills required to achieve a qualification determines its level. Level 2 is broadly equivalent to GCSE level (grades A*-C) and level 3 equates to GCE level. As you successfully achieve one level, you can then progress on to the next. BTEC qualifications are offered at Entry level, then levels 1, 2, 3, 4 and 5.

Learning and Skills Council (LSC)

The government body responsible for planning and funding education and training for everyone aged over 16 in England – except university students. You can find out more at www.lsc.gov.uk

Local Education Authority (LEA)

The local government body responsible for providing education for students of compulsory school age in your area.

Mentor

A more experienced person who will guide and counsel you if you have a problem or difficulty.

35

Mode of delivery

The way in which a qualification is offered to students, eg part-time, full-time, as a short course or by **distance learning**.

National Occupational Standard (NOS)

These are statements of the skills, knowledge and understanding you need to develop to be competent at a particular job. These are drawn up by the **Sector Skills Councils**.

National Qualification Framework (NQF)

The framework into which all accredited qualifications in the UK are placed. Each is awarded a level based on their difficulty which ensures that all those at the same level are of the same standard. (See also **levels of study**.)

National Vocational Qualification (NVQ)

Qualifications which concentrate upon the practical skills and knowledge required to do a job competently. They are usually assessed in the workplace and range from level 1 (the lowest) to level 5 (the highest).

Nested qualifications

Qualifications which have 'common' units, so that students can easily progress from one to another by adding on more units, such as the BTEC Award, BTEC Certificate and BTEC Diploma.

Pathway

All BTEC National qualifications are comprised of a small number of core units and a larger number of specialist units. These specialist units are grouped into different combinations to provide alternative pathways to achieving the qualification, linked to different career preferences.

Peer review

An occasion when you give feedback on the performance of other members in your team and they, in turn, comment on your performance.

Plagiarism

The practice of copying someone else's work and passing it off as your own. *This is strictly forbidden on all courses.*

Portfolio

A collection of work compiled by a student, usually as evidence of learning to produce for an **assessor**.

Professional body

An organisation that exists to promote or support a particular profession, such as the Law Society and the Royal Institute of British Architects.

Professional development and training

Activities that you can undertake, relevant to your job, that will increase and/or update your knowledge and skills.

Project

A comprehensive piece of work which normally involves original research and investigation either by an individual or a team. The findings and results may be presented in writing and summarised in a presentation.

Qualifications and Curriculum Authority (QCA)

The public body, sponsored by the **DfES**, responsible for maintaining and developing the national curriculum and associated assessments, tests and examinations. It also accredits and monitors qualifications in colleges and at work. You can find out more at www.qca.gov.uk

Quality assurance

In education, this is the process of continually checking that a course of study is meeting the specific requirements set down by the awarding body.

Sector Skills Councils (SSCs)

The 25 employer-led, independent organisations that are responsible for improving workforce skills in the UK by identifying skill gaps and improving learning in the workplace. Each council covers a different type of industry and develops its **National Occupational Standards**.

Semester

Many universities and colleges divide their academic year into two halves or semesters, one from September to January and one from February to July.

Seminar

A learning event between a group of students and a tutor. This may be student-led, following research into a topic which has been introduced earlier.

Specialist core units

See under **Core units**.

Study buddy

A person in your group or class who takes notes for you and keeps you informed of important developments if you are absent. You do the same in return.

Time-constrained assignment

An assessment you must complete within a fixed time limit.

Tutorial

An individual or small group meeting with your tutor at which you can discuss the work you are currently doing and other more general course issues. At an individual tutorial your progress on the course will be discussed and you can also raise any concerns or personal worries you have.

The University and Colleges Admissions Service (UCAS)

The central organisation which processes all applications for higher education courses. You pronounce this 'You-Cass'.

UCAS points

The number of points allocated by **UCAS** for the qualifications you have obtained. **HE** institutions specify how many points you need to be accepted on the courses they offer. You can find out more at www.ucas.com

Unit abstract

The summary at the start of each BTEC unit that tells you what the unit is about.

Unit content

Details about the topics covered by the unit and the knowledge and skills you need to complete it.

Unit points

The number of points you have gained when you complete a unit. These depend upon the grade you achieve (Pass, Merit or Distinction) and the size of the unit as determined by its **guided learning hours**.

Vocational qualification

A qualification which is designed to develop the specific knowledge and understanding relevant to a chosen area of work.

Work experience

Any time you spend on an employer's premises when you carry out work-based tasks as an employee but also learn about the enterprise and develop your skills and knowledge.

ACTIVITIES

This section focuses on grading criteria P5, P6, M4, D3, P7, M5, D4, P8 and M6. The activities included are specifically concerned with the cardiovascular system and respiratory system and how they respond to exercise. It also covers how the body uses its energy systems for different sport and exercise activities in this section of the guide.

Our cardiovascular and respiratory systems act as a delivery service, working together to supply oxygen to the energy systems. The energy systems then use this oxygen to produce energy for muscular contraction.

An understanding of the anatomy and physiology of each of these systems is imperative in the sport and exercise industries in order to begin to appreciate how the body copes with the stress of exercise, why we cannot continue to exercise indefinitely and how we can train these systems.

From the information studied in this Unit, the function of each system can be examined and applied to sport and exercise.

The full Unit explores the structure and function of the skeletal, muscular, cardiovascular and respiratory systems, and how each responds to exercise. We're going to look at the cardiovascular and respiratory systems in this Guide. To complete the Unit, each of the three energy systems is examined.

Learning outcomes

1 Understand the structure and function of the cardiovascular system and how it responds to exercise

2 Understand the structure and function of the respiratory system and how it responds to exercise

3 Understand the different energy systems and their use in sport and exercise.

Content

1) **Understand the structure and function of the cardiovascular system and how it responds to exercise**

Structure of the cardiovascular system: heart (atria, ventricles, bicuspid valve, tricuspid valve, chordae tendineae, aortic valve, pulmonary valve, aorta, superior vena cava, inferior vena cava, pulmonary vein, pulmonary artery); blood vessels (arteries, arterioles, capillaries, veins, venules)

Function of the cardiovascular system: delivery of oxygen and nutrients, removal of waste products, thermoregulation

Response to exercise: short term, eg anticipatory heart rate, heart rate at onset of exercise, redirection of blood flow (vasodilation and vasoconstriction); long term, eg cardiac hyptertrophy, increased stroke volume, increased cardiac output, decreased resting heart rate.

2) **Understand the structure and function of the respiratory system and how it responds to exercise**

Structure of the respiratory system: nasal cavity, pharynx, larynx, trachea, bronchus, bronchioles, lungs, alveoli, diaphragm, internal and external intercostal muscles

Function of the respiratory system: diffusion of oxygen into the blood stream, diffusion of carbon dioxide out of the blood stream

Mechanisms of breathing: inspiration and expiration

Respiratory volumes: eg tidal volume, inspiratory reserve volume, expiratory reserve volume, vital capacity, residual volume, total lung capacity

Response to exercise: short term, eg increased breathing rate, tidal volume; long term, eg increased vital capacity, increased strength of intercostal muscles.

3) **Understand the different energy systems and their use in sport and exercise**

Energy systems: creatine phosphate energy system; lactic acid energy system (anaerobic glycolysis, lactic acid production); aerobic energy system; amounts of ATP produced by each system; types of sports that use each system; recovery periods.

Grading criteria

P5 describe the structure and function of the cardiovascular system

You are required to describe the structure of the cardiovascular system. It is a good idea to include relevant diagrams of all the relevant parts together with an explanation of the function of each part.

P6 describe how the cardiovascular system responds to exercise

You need to describe the different changes that occur to your cardiovascular system when you exercise. You must explain both the short-term responses and the long-term adaptations.

M4 explain the function of the cardiovascular system and how it responds to exercise

For this criterion you are required to examine the cardiovascular system in more detail than P5. You need to explain how each of the structures is designed in a way that is specifically suited to its function. You must also explain the way in which the cardiovascular system responds to both short- and long-term exercise and why.

D3 analyse how the cardiovascular system responds to exercise

To meet D3 a detailed explanation of the specific long- and short-term responses of the cardiovascular system is needed. An analytical approach to aspects such as individual differences, the specific responses and adaptations to different intensities of exercise, different sporting disciplines, and exercises using different parts of the body is needed.

P7 describe the structure and function of the respiratory system, the mechanisms of breathing, respiratory volumes, and how the respiratory system responds to exercise

You are required to describe the structure of the respiratory system with an explanation of the functions of each of the identified parts. Describe the structures and movements involved in the breathing mechanism and also identify and explain the different respiratory volumes. Finally you are required to explain the long- and short-term changes of the respiratory system to exercise.

M5 explain the function of the respiratory system, including the mechanisms of breathing, and how it responds to exercise

The following criterion is an extension to P7. An explanation of how each of the structures of the system is designed to meet its function is required. You may wish to explain how breathing mechanisms and respiratory values change during exercise.

Also explain why the long- and short-term exercise responses take place.

D4 analyse how the respiratory system responds to exercise

D4 requires a detailed explanation of the specific long- and short-term responses of the respiratory system to exercise. An analytical approach to aspects such as the specific responses and adaptations to different types of exercise (eg aerobic, anaerobic), different sporting disciplines, and exercises using different parts of the body is needed. You may wish to address the limitations of responses due to anatomical differences and abnormalities.

P8 describe the different energy systems and their use in sport and exercise activities

You must describe the three energy systems (two anaerobic and one aerobic) and relate the energy systems to their use in different sport and exercise activities. Consider using a range of different sports activities to demonstrate your understanding of the intensity of the systems described.

M6 explain the different energy systems and their use in sport and exercise activities

You need to include a more detailed account of the energy systems than in P8 with an explanation of how they work. You may wish to describe how exercise demands change during sporting activities and how the recruitment of the three systems can alter as a result. Provide an explanation of the percentage of the energy system contribution to specific sport/exercise activities.

ACTIVITY 1

For this task you are required to use your own knowledge and research to insert the cardiac structures listed into their relevant position in the diagram.

left atrium

right atrium

left ventricle

right ventricle

bicuspid valve

tricuspid valve

chordae tendineae

aortic valve

pulmonary valve

aorta

superior vena cava

inferior vena cava

left pulmonary veins

right pulmonary veins

left pulmonary artery

right pulmonary artery

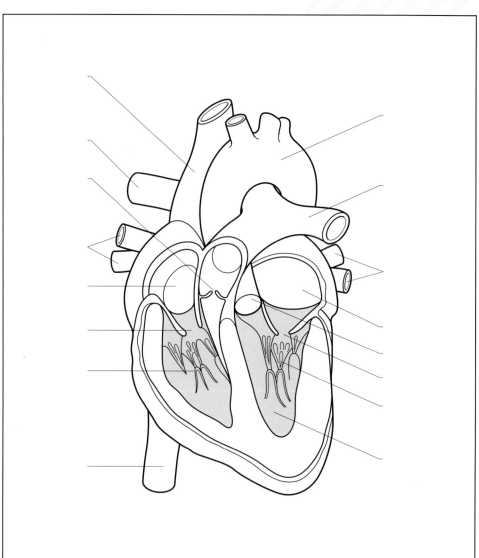

ACTIVITY 2

You need to know how blood flows through the double-loop circuit of the heart in the correct sequence.

Task 1

List the cardiovascular structures outlined below in the order in which the blood flows through them in the body:

Aortic valve	Pulmonary valve	Lungs
All areas of the body	Left ventricle	Left atrium
	Aorta	Bicuspid valve
Vena cava	Tricuspid valve	Pulmonary veins
Right atrium	Right ventricle	Pulmonary artery

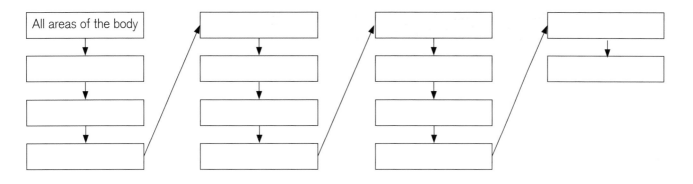

Task 2

For each point of the flow of blood through the body identify whether the blood will be oxygenated (red) or deoxygenated (blue).

Task 3

For each box on the diagram to the right, insert the correct structure and direction of blood flow.

Structures to be entered into the diagram

Lungs

Superior vena cava

Inferior vena cava

Right atrium

Left atrium

Left ventricle

Right ventricle

Capillaries

Venules

Veins

Arteries

Arterioles

Aorta

Pulmonary veins

Pulmonary artery.

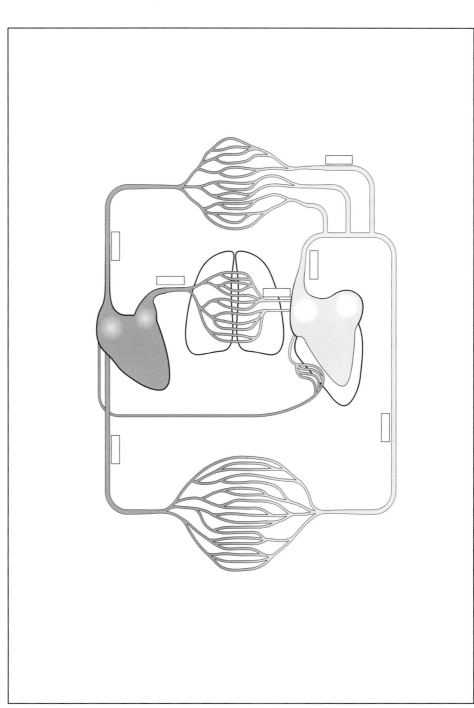

ACTIVITY 3

Below is a list of cardiovascular structures; unfortunately the definitions do not match the structures next to them. Match the structures to the correct definition using a line.

Veins

This valve is on the right side of the heart, between the right atrium and the right ventricle.

Bicuspid valve

Thread-like fibrous tissue attaching the tricuspid and bicuspid valves to the walls of the ventricles.

Tricuspid valve

These are large blood vessels. Many have one-way valves that prevent blood flowing backwards and causing it to pool due to gravity.

Aortic valve

Blood vessels with a small diameter, which extend branches from an artery to capillary beds.

Capillaries

Large blood vessels, containing a thick muscular wall, that carry blood away from the heart.

Chordae tendineae

Also known as the mitral valve and lies between the left atrium and the left ventricle.

Venules

Also called a semilunar valve, this has three half-moon-shaped cusps. While the heart contracts, pressure in the left ventricle rises and forces this valve open, allowing oxygenated blood to flow out of the heart and around the body.

Arterioles

The smallest blood vessels in the body, which allow gases to be transferred into and out of body tissues.

Arteries

Small blood vessel that allow blood to return from capillary beds.

ACTIVITY 4

On the next page is an image of the two largest types of blood vessel within the body. By looking at the images, and researching their structures and functions, identify the type of vessel shown. For each of these statements, say which vessel is being referred to:

- Has no pulse and blood travels under lower pressure (A/V)
- Contains valves (A/V)
- Has thick and elastic vessel walls (A/V)
- Mainly carries oxygenated blood (A/V)
- Returns blood to the heart (A/V)
- This vessel takes blood away from the heart (A/V)
- Has a pulse and blood travels under high pressure (A/V)
- Does not have valves (A/V)

- Walls of the vessel are thin (A/V)
- Mainly carries de-oxygenated blood (A/V)
- Has large lumen (A/V)
- Has small lumen (A/V)

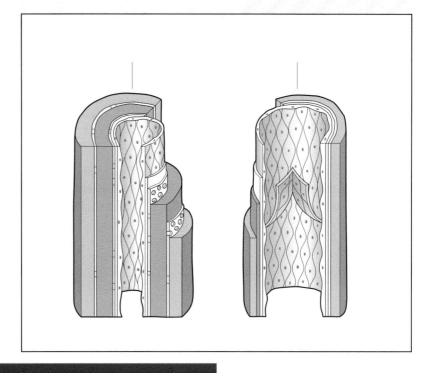

ACTIVITY 5

Task 1

In small groups, produce a poster that identifies the structures of the respiratory system. Include the following respiratory structures on your poster:

- Nasal cavity
- Pharynx
- Larynx
- Trachea
- Bronchus
- Bronchioles
- Lungs
- Alveoli
- Diaphragm
- Internal and external intercostal muscles.

For each of the structures, provide an explanation of their role.

On your poster include a description of the mechanical processes of inspiration and expiration and how the respiratory structures change during this process.

Task 2

On completing your poster, deliver a group presentation to explain the key structures in the respiratory system and how these structures work together to support the mechanisms of breathing.

ACTIVITY 6

The cardiovascular and respiratory systems can be studied as separate body systems. However, they must work together to supply oxygen and other nutrients, and remove carbon dioxide and other waste products, to enable physical activity and maintain general health.

Draw a stylised diagram of the human body and insert captions of how the cardiovascular and respiratory systems remove waste products, supply body parts with vital substances and maintain the body's homoeostasis (physiological balance). Consider the following:

- Delivery of oxygen and nutrients
- Removal of waste products
- Thermoregulation
- Diffusion of oxygen into the blood stream
- Diffusion of carbon dioxide out of the blood stream
- Diffusion of oxygen into the body tissues where it is needed
- Diffusion of carbon dioxide from the body tissues.

ACTIVITY 7

The following activity is designed to develop your understanding of the mechanical aspects of breathing and factors that can influence those aspects.

Task 1

Research and define the following terms related to respiratory volumes:

- Total lung capacity (TLC)
- Vital capacity (VC)
- Expiratory reserve volume (ERV)
- Residual volume (RV)
- Tidal volume (TV)
- Inspiratory reserve volume (IRV).

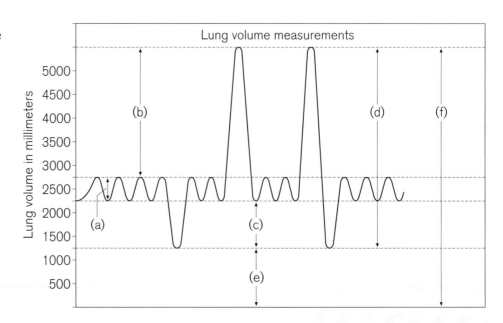

Task 2

A spirometer is a device used to measure lung volumes. The spirometer works by measuring the amount of air that we breathe in and out over a period of time and displaying the results in a graphical form. Above is a graph showing the type of readings that can be obtained by using a spirometer. With consideration of the definitions that you have obtained for Task 1, insert the six lung-volume terminologies into their correct place in the graph.

Task 3 (Extension activity)

- Explain the aspects that will contribute to individual differences in lung volume measures
- What will happen to the readings during exercise?
- Do large lung volumes necessarily mean that a person is fitter, and why?
- In what ways can these volumes influence the physical fitness and capabilities of different athletes?

ACTIVITY 8

Task 1

Design and implement a practical investigation into the short-term exercise responses of the cardiovascular and respiratory systems.

You must include an explanation of the method you will use, broken down into the following three sections:

- **Participants** – A simple explanation of the details of the individuals being tested in the experiment (eg age, gender, sporting background, employment etc)
- **Equipment** – A detailed list of all equipment that is needed to carry out your experiment
- **Procedure** – A clear explanation of how to carry out the investigation.

Select one of the examples outlined below for your experiment

- Use a heart rate monitor to investigate heart rate changes during varying intensities and types of exercise
- Test blood pressure changes in systolic and diastolic pressure during different types and intensities of exercise
- Measure body and or skin temperature to investigate the redirection of blood flow during exercise, through vasodilation and vasoconstriction
- Measure how breathing rate changes during different exercises
- Use a spirometer to measure the changes in lung volumes during exercise.

Tips:

- Take physical readings from your participants/s before, during and after exercise
- Investigate different types of exercise for comparison
- Test a range of people to make comparisons.

If you test more than person, make sure that you use identical procedures.

When you have collected the results, formulate these into a table and graphs and write an explanation of why the exercise responses have taken place.

Task 2 (Extension activity)

To demonstrate independent learning and reflective thought, this extension task requires you to analyse the results of your experiment. Consider the various factors that can influence your scientific experiment and the accuracy and validity of the data that you have collected.

ACTIVITY 9

Task 1

Design and carry out a training programme to develop your aerobic fitness/cardiovascular endurance. Make sure that you include the following aspects in your programme:

- Initial fitness tests and/or health tests to base your training levels at
- Implementation of the appropriate training principles:
    - FITT (frequency, intensity, time and type)
    - Specificity
    - Progression
    - Overload
- Fitness tests and/or health tests to check improvements.

Task 2

Think about how the results of your fitness tests have changed over time. Explain the physical long-term adaptations that have taken place to your cardiovascular and respiratory systems as a result of your training. Also, explain why these long-term adaptations have occurred.

Areas to consider:

- Increased vital capacity
- Increased strength of intercostal muscles
- Cardiac hypertrophy
- Increased stroke volume
- Increased cardiac output
- Decreased resting heart rate.

ACTIVITY 10

Sport and exercise activities require energy. The breakdown of the chemical adenosine triphosphate (ATP) provides us with the energy we need to exercise. As we only have very limited stores of ATP in our body we must regenerate it, using our energy systems, to continue exercising. The specific energy system that is used is determined by the intensity and duration of the exercise that is being performed. Our three energy systems are:

- ATP-CP system (creatine phosphate energy system)
- Lactic acid system (anaerobic glycolysis)
- Aerobic system (involving Krebs cycle)

Task 1

Research and summarise the characteristics of the three energy systems. Copy the table below and insert your findings.

Energy system	Amount of ATP produced	Duration of system	Exercise intensity	Speed of ATP production	Cause of fatigue
ATP-CP system					
Lactic acid system					
Aerobic system					

Task 2

Although there are three separate energy systems the body will often use more than one system at any time. This is particularly true when exercise demands are continuously changing (eg invasion games such as football, netball and rugby, etc). Sport and exercise activities can be seen as having different energy contributions rather than being exclusively related to one system. For the activities below, indicate your thoughts regarding the percentage energy system contribution.

Activity	ATP-CP system % contribution (high intensity)	Lactic acid system % contribution (moderate/ high intensity)	Aerobic system % contribution (moderate/ low intensity)
Middle distance running			
Football player			
Triathlon			
Dancer			
Boxing			
Marathon running			
Rugby			
Tennis			
Sprinting			
Cricket			

Task 3

Participate in a group discussion regarding the energy system contributions of different activities (how, when and why will energy system contributions change).

ANSWERS

ACTIVITY 2

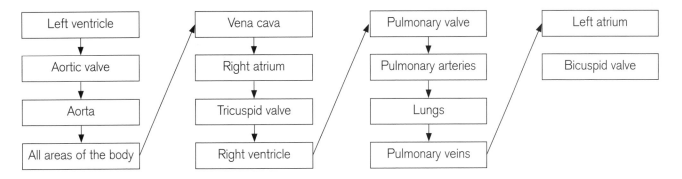

ACTIVITY 3

Veins

These are large blood vessels. Many have one-way valves that prevent blood flowing backwards and causing it to pool due to gravity.

Bicuspid valve

Also known as the mitral valve and lies between the left atrium and the left ventricle.

Tricuspid valve

This valve is on the right side of the heart, between the right atrium and the right ventricle.

Aortic valve

Also called a semilunar valve, this has three half-moon-shaped cusps. While the heart contracts pressure in the left vetricle rises and forces this valve open, allowing oxygenated blood to flow out of the heart and around the body.

Capillaries

The smallest blood vessels in the body, which allow gases to be transferred into and out of body tissues.

Chordae tendineae

Thread-like fibrous tissue attaching the tricuspid and bicuspid valves to the walls of the ventricles.

Venules

Small blood vessels that allow blood to return from capillary beds.

Arterioles

Blood vessels with a small diameter, which extend branches from an artery to capillary beds.

Arteries

Large blood vessels, containing a thick muscular wall, that carry blood away from the heart.

ACTIVITY 4

- Has thick and elastic vessel walls (A/V)
- This vessel takes blood away from the heart (A/V)
- Mainly carries oxygenated blood (A/V)
- Has small lumen (A/V)
- Has a pulse and blood travels under high pressure (A/V)
- Does not have valves (A/V)
- Returns blood to the heart (A/V)
- Walls of the vessel are thin (A/V)
- Mainly carries de-oxygenated blood (A/V)
- Has large lumen (A/V)
- Has no pulse and blood travels under lower pressure (A/V)
- Contains valves (A/V)

ACTIVITY 5

Part 1

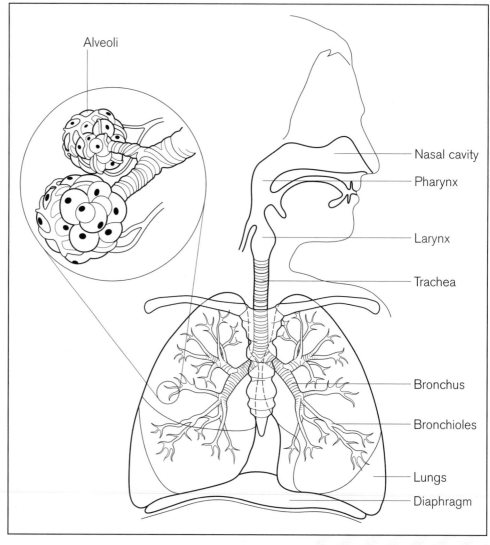

Explanation of their roles.

- Nasal cavity: is located above and behind the nose. It is filled with air and has the role of warming and filtering air as it is passed into the body and the respiratory system
- Pharynx: this is situated at the back of the mouth and nasal cavity. It is made up of different sections and it contains the epiglottis, which prevents food entering the respiratory system

- Larynx: this is often called the voice box and it contains the vocal chords enabling speech. It also protects the trachea

- Trachea: this often called the windpipe and is a bony tube that connects the nose and mouth to the lungs. This branches into two, and these become the bronchi

- Bronchus: there are two bronchi that branch off the trachea, one to each lung These allow the passage of gases in and out of lungs

- Bronchioles: small vessels that branch from the bronchi allowing gases to pass through as we breathe. Bronchioles are not surrounded by cartilage

- Lungs: large structures in the chest cavity that inflate and deflate during the breathing mechanism

- Alveoli: small sacks that resemble a bunch of grapes. This is where gas exchange takes place. CO2 is removed from the cardiovascular system as we breathe out and O2 is passed into the blood from the lungs via the alveoli

- Diaphragm: large sheet of muscle located at the bottom of the chest cavity and lungs. The diaphragm has a single tendon attached at the bottom that pulls downwards during inspiration, forcing air into the lungs due to atmospheric pressure

- Internal and external intercostal muscles: located between the ribs and assist with the mechanisms of breathing by contracting and relaxing during inspiration and expiration.

ACTIVITY 6

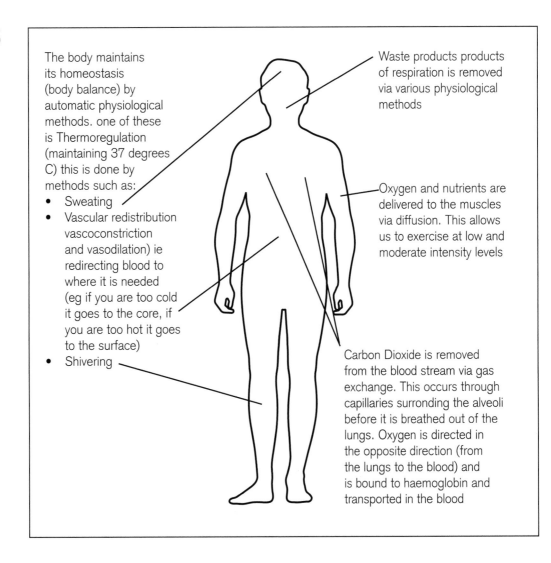

The body maintains its homeostasis (body balance) by automatic physiological methods. one of these is Thermoregulation (maintaining 37 degrees C) this is done by methods such as:
- Sweating
- Vascular redistribution vascoconstriction and vasodilation) ie redirecting blood to where it is needed (eg if you are too cold it goes to the core, if you are too hot it goes to the surface)
- Shivering

Waste products products of respiration is removed via various physiological methods

Oxygen and nutrients are delivered to the muscles via diffusion. This allows us to exercise at low and moderate intensity levels

Carbon Dioxide is removed from the blood stream via gas exchange. This occurs through capillaries surrounding the alveoli before it is breathed out of the lungs. Oxygen is directed in the opposite direction (from the lungs to the blood) and is bound to haemoglobin and transported in the blood

ACTIVITY 7

Part 1

- Total lung capacity (TLC): the volume of gas contained in the lung at the end of maximal inspiration
- Vital capacity (VC): the amount of air that can be forced out of the lungs after a maximal inspiration
- Expiratory reserve volume (ERV): the amount of additional air that can be breathed out after normal expiration
- Residual volume (RV): the amount of air left in the lungs after a maximal exhalation
- Tidal volume (TV): the amount of air breathed in or out during normal breathing
- Inspiratory reserve volume (IRV): the additional air that can be inhaled after a normal tidal breath in.

Part 2

a) Tidal volume (TV)

b) Inspiratory reserve volume (IRV)

c) Expiratory reserve volume (ERV)

d) Vital capacity (VC)

e) Residual volume (RV)

f) Total lung capacity (TLC)

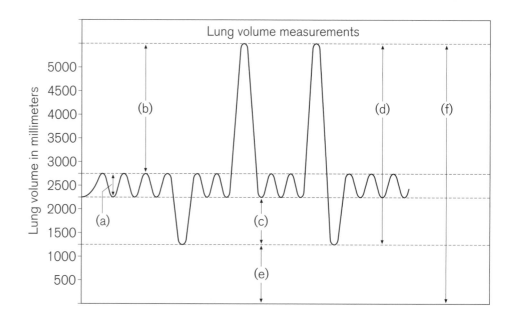

ACTIVITY 10

Part 1

Energy system	Amount of ATP produced	Duration of system	Exercise intensity	Speed of ATP production	Cause of fatigue
ATP-CP system	2 molecules	8–10 seconds	Very high	Very fast	Depletion of creatine stores
Lactic acid system	2 molecules	Up to 1 minute	High	Fast	Build up of lactic acid
Aerobic system	38 molecules	Indefinite	Moderate–low	Slow	Loss of glycogen/ glucose stores

Part 2

Activity	ATP-CP system % contribution (high intensity)	Lacticacidsystem % contribution (moderate/high intensity)	Aerobic system % contribution (moderate/low intensity)
Middle distance running	5	30	65
Football player	25	40	35
Triathlon	5	10	85
Dancer	33	33	33
Boxing	25	35	40
Marathon running	2	5	93
Rugby	30	30	40
Tennis	40	20	40
Sprinting	90	5	5
Cricket	30	10	60

These results may be different depending on a number of individual and situational factors. Variation in results will enable discussion in Part 3.

This section focuses on grading criteria P1, P2, P3, P4, P5; M1, M2, M3; D2 and aspects of P4 from Unit 4 'Sports Coaching'.

Learning outcomes

1 Know the key factors that influence health and safety in sport
2 Be able to carry out risk assessments
3 Know how to maintain the safety of participants and colleagues in a sports environment
4 Be able to plan a safe sporting activity.

Content

1) Know the key factors that influence health and safety in sport

Legislative factors: eg Health and Safety at Work Act (1974), additions to the (1974) Health and Safety at Work Act (Report of Injuries, Diseases and Dangerous Occurrences Regulation (RIDDOR)), Personal Protective Equipment 2002 (PPE), Control of Substances Hazardous to Health (COSHH), Health and Safety (First Aid) Regulations (1981), Manual Handling Operations Regulations (1992), Management of Health and Safety Regulations (1999), Fire and Safety of Places of Sports Act (1987), Adventurous Activities Licensing Act

Legal factors: law (statutory, civil law, case law); loco parentis; duty of care; higher duty of care; negligence

Regulatory bodies: appropriate to all activities (Health and Safety Executive (HSE), other regulatory bodies, eg local authorities, local educational authorities, police); appropriate to specific activities or specific types of activities, eg Adventurous Activities Licensing Authority (ALLA), governing bodies of sport.

2) Be able to carry out risk assessments

Risk assessments: aims (eliminate, minimise, protect participants from harm); objectives (identify hazards, identify those at risk, assess chance of hazard causing harm, grade risks); risk controls (eg do not do activity, modify activity, protect participants from hazard, provide appropriate safety equipment, provide appropriate training, provide appropriate supervisions for participants).

3) Know how to maintain the safety of participants and colleagues in a sports environment

Procedures: operating procedures and good practice, eg staff training, staff development, risk assessments, emergency procedure protocols, first aid, communications cascade system for notification of incidents; safety procedures and protocols, eg established to maintain a safe environment, governing body guidelines, equipment manufacturers guidelines, when to consult with others, who to consult with, local and national requirements.

4) Be able to plan a safe sporting activity

Plan: roles and responsibilities, eg leader, coaches, first aid; equipment (type, use); suitability of site; suitability of participants to activity; guidelines (participants, leaders); insurance

Review: eg effectiveness of risk management, injuries, near misses and dangerous occurrences, suitability of group for activity, effectiveness of briefings, suitability of equipment, support of other agencies (governing bodies, local authorities, police).

Grading criteria

P1 describe four legislative factors that influence health and safety in sport

This means that you will need to give details about four pieces of legislation from the above content. You must show some understanding of the importance of such legislation and point out how they influence health and safety in sport

M1 compare and contrast the influences of legislation, legal factors and regulatory bodies on health and safety in sport

This means that you will be able to make a link between legal definitions and the requirements of a good and responsible sports leader. You should be able to demonstrate a good knowledge of legislation, legal factors and regulatory bodies applied correctly to their chosen organisations

P2 describe the legal factors and regulatory bodies that influence health and safety in sport

This means that you must describe legal and regulatory terms, and regulatory bodies that define our behaviour and actions when working with others in a sporting environment

P3 carry out risk assessments for two different sports activities, with support

To successfully achieve this grading criterion you must complete two risk assessments with sporting activities, with teacher support. These risk assessments must include aims and controls to eliminate and minimise and protect participants from harm

M2 carry out risk assessments for two different sports activities

To achieve this specific criterion all learners must complete two risk assessments independently. The risk assessments must include the appropriate risk controls

P4 describe three procedures used to promote and maintain a healthy and safe sporting environment

To successfully achieve this grading criterion you must describe three procedures that are used to ensure good practice in maintaining health and safety of participants and colleagues in a sports environment

M3 explain three procedures used to promote and maintain a healthy and safe sporting environment

To successfully achieve this grading criterion you must explain three procedures that are used to ensure good practice in maintaining health and safety of participants and colleagues in a sports environment

D2 analyse three procedures used to promote and maintain a healthy and safe sporting environment

To successfully achieve this grading criterion you must analyse three procedures that are used to ensure good practice in maintaining health and safety of participants and colleagues in a sports environment

P5 produce a plan for the safe delivery of a selected sports activity and review the plan

To achieve this grade you could link it to Unit 4, Sports coaching. Place yourself in the role of a sports coach who is organising a coaching session for a group of athletes in a selected sport. Produce the plan that will enable the coach to deliver an effective coaching session in a safe environment. The plan you produce could be for the coaching session you are required to deliver in Unit 4: Sports Coaching Outcome 3: P4 plan a sports coaching session. Following your coaching session, you could review the health and safety plan through a series of reflective questions on a review sheet, eg were the activities suitable for the students' level of ability?

M4 explain the plan for the safe delivery of a selected sports activity and review the plan

Having produced your health and safety plan and achieving P5, you need to add a written piece of work explaining why these areas are being addressed for this particular coaching session, eg why a plan might have strict guidelines on protocols and procedures for participants in a trampoline session.

Explain the review questions and answers, saying why it is important a review takes place

D3 identify strengths and areas for improvement in the plan, suggesting how it could be improved

Having reviewed the plan, you now need to highlight the strengths and identify the weaknesses, saying why they were weak and what you would do differently next time to make the plan more effective.

ACTIVITY 1 (P1)

Task 1

The Health and Safety at Work Act 1974

The main aim of this Act is to make you aware of the importance of health and safety in the workplace, whether you are a manager, the owner of a business, a company employee or indeed anyone involved in the workplace.

Case study

Mark is looking forward to two weeks' work experience at his local leisure centre. Mark has visited the centre many times before for various sporting activities but is looking forward to experiencing the challenge of meeting customer needs in a leisure environment. Upon his arrival Mark notices that in the staffroom there are no health and safety guidelines for staff to follow. His tutor particularly asked him to look for these guidelines. Upon asking the centre manager for more information about health and safety guidelines the manager asked Mark to assist in designing staffroom notices that were in the process of being re-written.

Mark must therefore research and gather the necessary information before designing the new notices.

The following are headings, which will assist Mark in his work:

- Employer's responsibilities under the Health and Safety at Work Act (HSWA)
- Employee's responsibility under the HSWA
- Enforcement under the Health and Safety law
- The organisation's Health and Safety Policy.

Complete the following tables, describing the responsibilities of each of the four above headings:

Responsibilities of the employer under the HSWA
1 To give all employees training in regards to health and safety in the workplace and provide relevant information.
2
3
4

Responsibilities of the employee under the HSWA

1 It is the responsibility of the employee not to misuse equipment that has been provided for their own health and safety.

2

3

4

Enforcement of Health and Safety law

1 Health and Safety inspectors can enter the premises at any time to inspect the facility, eg take photographs, test equipment, etc.

2

3

4

The organisation's Health and Safety Policy

1 Who has been appointed to be responsible for Health and Safety in the workplace?

2

3

4

Task 2

The manager has asked Mark and his colleagues to make a short presentation to the rest of the leisure centre staff describing the Health and Safety at Work Act (1974) using the information he has researched above. Prepare Mark's presentation.

ACTIVITY 2

THE FIRE SAFETY AND SAFETY OF PLACES OF SPORT ACT 1987

Fans killed in football stadium fire

At least 70 people have died, and hundreds more have been injured, as a result of a fire at the Smallville United football stadium.

As people rushed to escape the blaze, many were crushed to death, mainly children and the elderly. Many more are being treated in hospital for burns.

'The fire spread so quickly', said one survivor, 'and the smoke was dreadful, we were all choking. It is such a tragedy that so many have lost their lives.'

(fictional account)

The Safety of Sports Grounds Acts 1975 was to ensure the safety of spectators by requiring the owners and organisers of premises to have a certificate of safety issued by the local authority. There are two types of certificates awarded: one which covers sport and recreational activities for an indefinite period of time and one issued for special events such as one-off concerts.

Task 1

Summarise the main recommendations of the Popplewell Report.

Describe the Act that was a direct result of the Popplewell Report.

What was the most relevant part of the Act for sports grounds?

Describe by giving examples the type of information that would be required for a General Safety Certificate.

Over the years there have been incidents like that at the fictional Smallville United football ground mentioned above. In small groups, research the problems that existed at these sports grounds, which resulted in so many fatalities. Share your findings with each group.

Task 2

Working in sport and sports activities presents a level of risk to employers and those partaking in the activities.

The Health and Safety (First Aid) Regulations (1981) is very important for those working in sports and providing sporting activities to understand and to use the correct procedures regarding first aid.

Try to visit a local football ground. This could be at your local leisure centre, a semi-professional football ground or your local professional club.

Copy and complete the following table:

Name of ground	
Identify the first aid room(s).	
Describe the first aid room and its contents.	
How many first aiders are present at training sessions and matches?	
Where are the first aid boxes?	
Describe the contents of the first aid boxes.	

Working in groups, describe what is in place at the football ground that could deal with an emergency.

ACTIVITY 3

REPORTING INJURIES, DISEASES AND DANGEROUS OCCURRENCES REGULATIONS 1995 (RIDDOR)

You are working as a lifeguard at a leisure centre. It is a very quiet evening and there are few swimmers in the pool. Billy, an elderly gentleman who swims every evening, is there as usual. He usually swims 20 lengths and then says a quick goodnight to whoever is on duty. Tonight on his way over to you Billy appears to stumble and fall. You are not certain what has caused the fall but as he falls he bangs his head. You have just had a training session on the reporting of accidents or dangerous incidents that might occur in the swimming pool so you know the procedure to follow.

After dealing with the incident you must complete an Incident Report Form.

Task 1

Copy and complete the Incident Report Form overleaf:

Incident Report Form

Club/centre/organisation

Your name

Date of report

The date and time of the incident/injury

Name of the person involved in the incident/injury

Contact details of the person involved in the incident/injury

Description of the incident/injury

Details of any injury
Outline what action was taken.

What onsite first aid was given?

What emergency service support was needed?

Details of any witnesses

Was evacuation necessary?

Details of the present situation regarding the injured person/incident and any additional information

Task 2

Describe this regulation that influences health and safety in sport and say why you think it is important to complete an incident report form.

Task 3

Your employer has a legal duty under RIDDOR that requires them to report and record some work-related accidents.

Form into small groups. Each group should look at one of the categories in the following table:

Deaths and major injuries

What is reportable under RIDDOR	
Deaths	If there is an accident that results in a death in the pool, who must be informed?
Major injuries	Give examples of reportable major injuries that may occur in the swimming pool.
Reportable diseases	Give an example of a disease that may need to be reported.
A reportable dangerous occurrence	Describe what is meant by a dangerous occurrence. What type of dangerous occurrence may you find in a swimming pool?

Working in small groups, each group will research one of the following, but ensure that all the topics are covered. The groups should present their findings to the rest of the class.

a) What records must be kept of any reportable injury, disease or dangerous occurrence in a sports complex?

b) How might the records be kept?

c) What do you understand by the words 'Incident Contact Centre' (ICC)?

d) How does the ICC work?

You may find the following website useful in your research:

www.hse.gov.uk/riddor/guidance.htm

ACTIVITY 4

CONTROL OF SUBSTANCES HAZARDOUS TO HEALTH (COSHH)

Task 1

Draw a basic plan/overview of a sports facility that you are familiar with. It may be a small complex or it may include a swimming pool, grass pitches, grass tennis courts, a sports hall, showers, changing areas, etc. On your plan/overview identify possible examples of hazardous substances that will be used to maintain the day-to-day running of the facility.

For example:

A swimming pool will use chemicals in the water and cleaning materials to clean the showers and toilets.

A grass football pitch will use fertiliser and substances to mark the white lines.

Create a table like the one overleaf, and list all of the substances that you have identified on your facility overview.

Substances	What they are used for	Level of risk Low/Medium/High

Task 2

Many substances have the potential to cause harm. Describe what employers are required to do to avoid the above substances being hazardous to health.

State why it is important that employers should pass on information and knowledge about hazardous substances to their employees.

ACTIVITY 5

PERSONAL PROTECTIVE EQUIPMENT AT WORK REGULATION 1992 (PPE)

Task 1

You are required to wear personal protective equipment for some of your daily tasks within a sports complex. Identify and describe the protection you might wear and explain why it is important to wear this protection. (Think about the tasks that you might undertake in a sports complex: eg a climbing instructor, a pool supervisor working with chemicals, a cleaner.)

Task 2

How might the regulations affect you if you are asked to work with a computer at a sports complex? Create and fill in a table like the one below.

List problems that could relate to the use of a computer monitor for long	periods What can the employer do to reduce the risk of problems arising?
1 Headaches	1 Free eyesight test provided
2	2
3	3
4	4
5	5

ACTIVITY 6 (P2)

You are a sports journalist employed by your local evening newspaper. There are often sports-related newsworthy stories to publish. Select three of your past reports and print the headline and the opening paragraph, describing the story. Say which laws and regulations are related to each story.

Example headline 1:

Worker injured at Leisure Complex – no first aider on duty

Example headline 2:

Participant at Leisure Centre slips on wet floor – no warning notices

Example headline 3:

Participant claims damage for back injury which has left him wheel-chair bound

ACTIVITY 7

Case study

Mr and Mrs Barker have paid for their daughter to take part in a fun day at a private health club. These days are organised during school holidays and held on sports fields at the nearby comprehensive school. Mr and Mrs Barker have left Anna in your care and signed a slip giving her permission to attend the day. You and the organisers are *in loco parentis*.

1) Describe what *in loco parentis* means.

2) What are your legal responsibilities?

ACTIVITY 8

If you are managing a sports or leisure complex you have a duty of care for the health and safety of anyone who may be affected by your actions at work should you fail to implement the correct duty of care procedures.

1) List five examples of people who may be affected by your actions if you are employed in sport or leisure. For example:

   a) Sports coaches who have not been briefed on the leisure centre's health and safety policies.

ACTIVITY 9

Mr O'Connor runs a private health and fitness club. There are two promotional open weekends a year. Several coaches are taking exhibition classes. You have been asked to run an exhibition football match for 9–11 year olds during school holidays. The club runs fun weeks and Mr O'Connor is keen to attract boys and girls of this age group for the next fun week. Mr O'Connor has organised the weekend events and although it is also your responsibility the duty of care falls heavily on the shoulders of the organiser.

Task 1

Describe what is meant by 'duty of care'. The following words or terms may assist you. You will need to define the following terms in order to help you complete this task.

- Legal and moral duty
- Suing in a court of law
- Safe
- Participant
- Spectator
- Efficient
- Injured
- Seek compensation
- Damages.

> During the game a child is fouled and falls. Reaching forward, the child protects herself but cuts her hand badly on glass on the pitch. The coach had quickly looked over the pitch before the commencement of the game. The child has damaged a tendon and her parents plan to seek compensation by suing in a court of law.

Task 2

What three points will need proving for the legal action to succeed?

Divide into three groups.

Group 1: prepare a statement trying to prove negligence. Consider if the event organiser was at fault in failing to meet a reasonable standard of care. You must establish the following:

a) The defendant owed a duty of care

b) The defendant breached that duty of care

c) The child suffered damage because the defendant breached that duty of care.

Group 2: prepare a statement in defence of Mr O'Connor and the coach.

a) Could the coach have been reasonably expected to explore every square metre of the pitch before the game?

b) Were there procedures to prevent sharp objects from being thrown onto the pitch?

c) Were there enough safety measures in place?

Group 3: discuss the scenario from both sides while groups 1 and 2 are preparing their statements. Listen to their statements. Take the role of the judge and decide if the organiser was negligent and liable to pay damages to the injured child. Did the event organiser act as responsibly as any other person would act under the same circumstances?

ACTIVITY 10

HIGHER DUTY OF CARE

Thousands of school trips take place every year and teachers/tutors have the responsibility of care for all the students who go on school trips – some of which involve potentially dangerous activities. It is therefore important that there is an adequate teacher/tutor:student ratio.

A schoolteacher was convicted of manslaughter of a pupil who drowned while on a school trip.

In groups, research sports-related educational cases where there have been tragic accidents. Present your findings to the other groups. Complete your presentations by summarising why the judgements were given for each case and state whether your group agrees or disagrees with the conclusions. Give reasons for your statements.

ACTIVITY 11

REGULATORY BODIES THAT INFLUENCE HEALTH AND SAFETY IN SPORT

No sporting activity can be made completely risk free. Sports' national governing bodies and their associated clubs and societies are legally responsible for ensuring that procedures are developed that will lessen the impact of external or internal risk factors on athletes, spectators, public, coaches or anyone involved in any form of sporting activity.

The **Health and Safety Act at Work Act 1974** provided for the formation of specific bodies to monitor and regulate health and safety at work.

1) Describe the role of the Health and Safety Commission.

The Health and Safety Executive investigates serious injuries or deaths that occur at work in facilities such as sports complexes. What other tasks are undertaken by the Health and Safety Executive? An example has been provided.

1) Inspect workplace – describe using sentences

2) In small groups, select one of the following regulatory bodies and research how that body ensures that appropriate health and safety regulations and codes of practice are fully implemented. Make sure that all of these bodies are covered between the groups.

- Local authorities
- The Sports Council
- The National Training Organisation for Sport, Recreation and Allied Occupations (SPRITO)
- The Central Council of Physical Recreation (CCPR)
- The Institute of Sport and Recreation.

Design a leaflet that describes clearly the work of the regulatory body you have researched.

ACTIVITY 12

ADVENTUROUS ACTIVITIES LICENSING ACT

From Lyme Bay to licensing

Past, present and future – the development of current regulation of outdoor adventure activities

The deaths of the four teenagers in the Lyme Bay canoeing tragedy in March 1993 will be remembered for a very long time by many people, not only family and friends, but also those involved in the outdoor activity community.

The canoeing tragedy was the result of circumstances, which the Devon County Council report states 'quite simply, should not have happened.' This report goes on to say that 'the immediate cause of the tragedy was, however, the lamentable failure of the St Alban's Centre to organise and supervise the canoeing activity, to employ suitable staff and to have prepared and operated sensible and pre-determined procedures when difficulties arose.' The successful prosecution of the parent company, OLL and the managing director, Peter Kite, was based around these issues.

(www.bbc.co.uk)

1) Investigate this tragedy further and describe the key factors that brought about the Adventurous Activities Licensing Act (AALA).
2) What is the aim of the AALA?
3) Describe a sample of the licensable activities that are included in the Act.

ACTIVITY 13

NATIONAL GOVERNING BODIES

Produce and complete a table like this one.

What is every sport represented by?	
NGBs identify risks within their sport to clubs and societies. What could happen if they failed to do so? Eg what would happen if there was an accident involving a spectator?	
Do NGBs have sole responsibilities for Health and Safety within their sports? Who else has responsibility to comply with laws and rules?	
What is the primary responsibility of the NGB?	
The Health and Safety at Work Act creates obligations that apply to activities within certain clubs. What are those obligations?	Statutory – explain
What duty applies to club officers, committees, members, coaches to take responsible care not to cause damage or injury to others	Common law duty – explain

ACTIVITY 14 (M1)

For a sports magazine, write an article that compares and contrasts the influences of the following on health and safety:

- Legislation
- Legal factors
- Regulatory bodies.

ACTIVITY 15 (P3 AND M2)

RISK ASSESSMENTS

Most sports have some forms of procedure in place to control and minimise the chances of accidents occurring.

Scenario: the sports college which you attend has asked the group to provide a wall chart that fully covers how to carry out risk assessments. The wall chart must be attractive and informative. Many students in the college assist at local sports clubs and, as part of the sports studies course, plan and deliver sessions, organise events, etc. Some have part-time jobs at leisure centres. Therefore risk assessments can be based on your – and their – own experiences.

The wall chart should have pockets for exemplar material, leaflets, forms and examples of risk assessments.

Task 1

As a group, discuss and design an attractive title for the wall chart, which identifies the aims of a risk assessment.

Task 2

All students should be familiar with the terminology used in risk assessments. Working in small groups, describe the following:

a) *Hazard*. Give three examples of hazards in a sports environment. How is each example a hazard and to whom?

b) *Risk*. Give three examples of risks in a sporting environment and explain how each example is a risk and to whom.

c) *Risk assessment*. Explain the meaning of the term 'risk assessment'.

Add your descriptions to the wall chart.

Task 3

Risk assessments identify the following:

- Facilities, equipment and activities involved
- Hazards associated with these facilities, equipment and activities
- People directly or indirectly affected by those hazards
- Levels of risk experienced by those people exposed to the hazards
- Measures put in place to reduce the risks to acceptable levels.

Choose an example of an event/activity in which you have been involved and identify the following:

- Facilities, equipment and the event/activity
- Identify the hazards (something that has the potential to cause harm)
- Who might be harmed (identify those at risk)
- Assess the risk (estimate and evaluate the risk on a scale of 1–3)
- Grade the risk (low, medium, high or unlikely, possible, probable).

Show examples of this work on the wall chart.

Task 4 (P3 and M2)

It is very important when working through the risk assessment process to reduce the risks of the sport to acceptable levels.

Here is an example from the Royal Yachting Association of a generic risk assessment for medium risk events.

Case study C: Generic risk assessment proforma

Royal Yachting Association (www.rya.org.uk)

Extract from 'The RYA generic risk assessment for Medium events'

The Medium Event model is similar in structure to the Major Event model, but with fewer risk control measures in place and no reference to crisis management plans. It is anticipated that an annual assessment could be carried out, and used for any event run by a club. Clearly if a club were to run cruiser racing, as well as dinghy and windsurfing racing, the different nature of the risks in each case might require different risk assessments forms for each kind of vessel involved.

1 Measures	General comments	Applicability
1 Planning		
1.1 Use of Tidal Prediction Information	Time events to suit tidal range & streams	
1.2 Limit Competitor Numbers	Match entry numbers to resources	
1.3 Planning of Starting Sequence	Separate classes and avoid risk of collision	
1.4 Advance Briefing of Race Management	By oral briefing and/or written instructions	
1.5 Advance Safety Briefing with Authorities	Liaise with relevant port and safety organisations	
1.6 Shipping Movement Monitoring	Obtaining details of movements from Port Control	
1.7 Weather Monitoring	Use forecasts to decide whether to proceed	
1.8 Manning	Ensure competent personnel for race management	
1.9 Emergency/Contingency Procedures	Establishment of action plan for emergencies	
1.10 Media Management	One contact to control information fed to media in an emergency	
1.11 Race Management Team Welfare	Ensure race management volunteers are equipped for the event	
2 Communications		
2.1 Notice of Race	Specify conditions and safety requirements to competitors	
2.2 Notice of Race	Include compliance with Harbour Bylaws	
2.3 Safety Briefing	Safety briefing to Competitors	
2.4 Competitors' Shore Contact	Record details of all crew members on board	
2.5 Shore Signals	Race Signals as provided under the RRS	
2.6 VHP Radio Announcements	Designated VHP channel for announcements	
2.7 Communications with Authorities	Port control	
2.8 Mobile Telephones and VHP	Port control	
2.9 International Collision Regulations	For right of way between racing and non-racing traffic	

1 Measures	General comments	Applicability
3 Control Measures Before Start		
3.1 Safety Inspections	Spot checks of on-board safety equipment	
3.2 Marshalling and Patrol Boats	Safety craft for traffic control during starts and at finish	
3.3 Competitor Marshalling Areas	Designated areas for waiting in event of traffic	
3.4 Postponement/suspension of Starts	In the event of commercial or other traffic movements	
3.5 Length of Starting Line	Matched to competitor numbers per RYA recommendations	
3.6 Ferry Traffic	Check ferry times on race date and avoid traffic dash	
4 Additional Control Measures After Start and During Race		
4.1 Abandonment	In the event of adverse weather or other factors	
4.2 Shortening Course	In the event of lack of wind or other factors	
4.3 Race Observers	Observers on shore at strategic locations	
4.4 Escort vessels	Club member's or other vessels	
4.5 Monitoring of Wind/sea Conditions	By communication with observers and escort vessels	
5 Additional Control Measures at Finish		
5.1 Finishing Line Length	Matched to number/size of competing boats	
5.2 Retirement Monitoring	Reporting by boats retiring or tally system	
5.3 Harbour Patrol	Patrolling of finishing area	
5.4 Race Declaration	Boats sign in after race to monitor all finishers	
5.5 Use of Engine	Boats to clear line after crossing the finishing line	
6 Special Control Measures		
6.1		
6.2		

Create a similar table for a sport of your choice that you consider to be 'medium risk'. You may have support from your tutor if you wish.

Mount examples of the risk assessments on the wall chart.

ACTIVITY 16

RISK CONTROLS

You are leading a Duke of Edinburgh's Award Scheme activity. It has been planned for many weeks and you have an overnight stay in tents on the North Yorkshire Moors. You are watching the weather forecast very carefully. Copy the table below and choose one activity from the following:

- Climbing
- Canoeing
- Map and compass work.

Complete the table.

What circumstances (hazards) might arise that would lead you to decide to cancel the activity?	Circumstances such as …
What circumstances (hazards) might arise during the trip, which would lead you to modify the activity either before or during the trip?	Circumstances such as …
How might you protect the participants from potential hazards?	
What appropriate safety equipment might you provide?	

ACTIVITY 17

The Duke of Edinburgh's Award Scheme includes many different sporting activities.

A general guide could be produced for those who are due to take part in such activities.

In small groups, create a simple guide.

Within your group, select four sporting activities and give instructions on how having the correct equipment could control risks for certain activities. Give examples of equipment and describe how this equipment eliminates or reduces possible risks.

There should be a section in your guide about first aid. If you were to lead a group on one of these activities, what first aid training would you need someone to have within the group?

Many college students assist at clubs. Write a short article for the guide discussing the obligation that managers at the clubs have to use coaches with specific training qualifications for the various activities.

Have you ever had the experience of assisting at a sports session and being left in charge without adequate training? What would be the consequences should there be an accident? Write a few guidance notes for students should this situation arise.

Finally in the guide you are asked to give guidance about appropriate supervision of participants. Select examples of activities and state what ratio of supervisors to participants would be needed for these activities.

ACTIVITY 18 (P3, M2)

Using your college proforma, complete a risk assessment as an example for the guide for a Duke of Edinburgh's Award activity with which you are to assist. You may have support from your leader.

Now review the controls in the risk assessment that you have carried out.

■ Evaluate how effective these controls will be in eliminating and reducing risk.

■ Evaluate how effective the controls will be in protecting people from that risk.

ACTIVITY 19 (P3, M2)

Combine this activity with a practical session that you might deliver to other students or a specific selected group.

Using the Risk Assessment form used by your organisation would you complete a Risk Assessment for the practical session you will to deliver?

The risk assessment may be completed with or without the support of your teacher.

D1

On completion of the session, review the risk assessment controls and evaluate their effectiveness.

ACTIVITY 20

Task 1 (P4)

There is a job advertisement in the local newspaper.

> **Summer Sports Events for young people**
> **8 – 14 years old**
>
> Sports coaches and supervisors needed
>
> Summer Sports Programme July 26 – August 30
>
> Applications and details from
>
> Director of Sport, County Hall
>
> Closing date: 22 June
>
> Telephone: 01482 86316
>
> Applicants must have knowledge of health and safety procedures

Write a letter of application and include a brief paragraph showing that you have knowledge of procedures used to promote and maintain a healthy and safe sporting environment.

Task 2

You receive a letter calling you for an interview. At the interview, it is stated that you will be asked questions about procedures regarding the issue of first aid.

Plan a mock interview with a partner and think carefully about questions you might be asked.

Your partner prepares the following questions. Provide the answers:

1) What course have you covered which would enable you to work with us as a fist aider?

2) Describe the main points of the course for me.

3) Do you have the qualities that make a good first aider? What are those qualities?

4) If we were to appoint you as a first aider, could you fulfil other roles also?

5) We provide many different sporting activities at several venues. There is a good first aid room at the leisure complex but not at some of the locations we use. How would you overcome not having access to a first aid room?

6) What do you know about portable first aid kits? Give examples of what the regulations do not allow you to carry.

7) Could you tell me what I need to consider when organising the summer events in order to fulfil the requirements of the Health and Safety Regulations 1981?

   (eg the risks and hazards to young people, the number of young people taking part in activities)

ACTIVITY 21 (P4)

You are really pleased when a letter arrives appointing you as a supervisor for the summer events programme. For the first two weeks you are supervising the registration, changing, equipment etc along with a qualified athletics coach. You are working at the main sports complex accessing indoor and outdoor facilities.

The coach informs you that there is going to be a practice fire drill that afternoon during one of the indoor sessions. He asks you to check over the emergency procedures at the sports complex. You return with the information requested.

Answer the following questions:

1) What emergency situations could arise during an indoor athletics session?

2) Describe exactly where there is the means for fighting a fire should there be one. Show this on a simple plan.

3) Through which doors will you and the coach guide the young people during the fire drill? Show the route on a plan.

4) Why would you instruct the students not to put equipment in front of exit doors?

5) In which direction do you think these doors will open?

6) When explaining to the students about the fire drill, describe the main points you would talk about.

7) You know that there is a fire drill in the afternoon; however, do you know what to do if you discover a fire? Go to the reception desk and ask them for the standard operating procedure for dealing with a fire. Write this out on an A4 sheet of paper for the coach to access easily.

ACTIVITY 22 (P4)

At the end of the five weeks you have done so well you are offered a weekend job at the sports complex. Your first weekend is to be spent training. This means that you have to report back to other young members of staff the content of the training weekend. Your task is to describe a specific Health and Safety issue in the form of a short presentation. You decide to select the issue regarding the safety procedure and protocol established to maintain a safe sports' environment.

Take photographs, draw simple plans, show leaflets and posters which already exist, and provide contact addresses and numbers that may be useful to anyone involved in maintaining a safe environment for participants and colleagues to assist you with your presentation.

You have the following headings from your training weekend to assist you:

- The safety programmes involved in the inspecting of facilities and equipment
- The manufacturer's guidelines on the use of equipment
- How the safety programme is evaluated and monitored
- The training and development of staff regarding health and safety
- Local and national requirements regarding health and safety.

Describe in detail the safety procedures and protocols established at the sports complex to maintain a safe environment.

ACTIVITY 23 (M3)

Having completed activities 20, 21 and 22, use these findings to complete the following task.

You have now worked at the sports complex for six months and you are expected to know a wide range of procedures and protocols for maintaining the safety of participants and colleagues. The sports centre is having an open day and would like you to assist with the preparation.

With a colleague, prepare a display that explains to the public a wide range of procedures for maintaining the safety of participants and colleagues. This display may be in the form of photographs, detailed written information, posters, use of equipment, notices, guidelines etc.

Through the display, ensure that you explain in detail three procedures used in the sports complex to promote and maintain a healthy and safe sporting environment.

ACTIVITY 24 (D2)

As well as the display, you are to produce a short video or written report. Through the video, analyse three procedures used to promote and maintain a healthy and safe sporting environment in the sports centre. The video or report could be based at your college/school or any leisure facility you have access to.

Consider all the factors you have learned from the previous activities.

For example:

- Emergency procedures
- Reporting accidents
- Health and Safety regulations
- First aid – first aiders
- Training and staff development
- Manufacturers guidelines for the use of equipment.

In this section there will be a number of activities for you to complete. These will help you understand what you need to do to successfully achieve the grading criteria for Learning outcome 4.

Activities 25–27 cover P5, M4 and D3.

ACTIVITY 25

BE ABLE TO PLAN A SAFE SPORTING ACTIVITY

All sports coaches have a duty of care to the participants with a priority given to health and safety issues. The aim of the coach is to reduce the risk of incidents and make the performance arena safer for participants. To achieve this, the coach needs to have thorough planning in place for an effective safe session.

In pairs, assume the role of a coach. This coming Saturday you have 10 boys and 10 girls, 12–14 years old, of mixed ability, attending a sports day organised by you.

Produce an initial draft plan:

Task 1

- Select a safe and appropriate venue for your sports day. This could be a local leisure centre, swimming pool, private facility or a sports facility at your school or college
- Produce a risk assessment for the facility and session. Use the previous activities in this Unit and Unit 4: Sports Coaching, to help you in this task.

Task 2

- Select activities appropriate to the participants' profile, making sure they are safe with no foreseeable problems likely to occur, eg injuries caused by lack of fitness or poor technique due to the level of performer
- Produce an equipment list with all equipment being safe and appropriate to the session; eg if you choose to incorporate cricket,

do you use a cricket ball with pads, helmet, gloves etc or a tennis ball due to the participants' profile?

Task 3

- Produce emergency accident procedures for participants. Guidelines should cover all foreseeable emergencies, eg fire, illness, injury
- Identify coaches' roles and responsibilities, taking into account coaching and health and safety responsibilities; eg who is responsible for which activities, who is responsible for first aid
- Produce emergency accident procedures for the coaches – accident reporting, fire, first aid procedures.

ACTIVITY 26

Present all areas of your initial plan to the class and discuss, gaining feedback and input from the group as to the effectiveness of the plan for the safe delivery of the sports day.

Create a table like the one below, and take notes highlighting the strengths and weaknesses and ideas from the class, as these could be added to your final plan.

Strengths	Weaknesses

ACTIVITY 27

From your class discussion you should now produce your final plan for the sports day, taking into account the points you have covered in Activities 26 and 27, as well as the information you have gathered from the activities throughout this Unit and the knowledge you have gained from Unit 4: Sports Coaching.

ACTIVITY 28

HEALTH AND SAFETY SPORTS DAY REVIEW

As a coach it is an important consideration to be continually reflective regarding the events and activities that you organise. This can be carried out prior to, during and after the event has taken place. For this activity, you are required to fill in a review checklist regarding the planning and operations involved in your event.

Checklist prior to the event

	Yes	No	Action	Comments
Has a detailed and appropriate risk assessment been carried out?				
Is theresufficient first aid provision for the event?				
Is the group involved at a suitable level for the planned activities?				
Has a detailed equipment check been completed and appropriateness of the equipment been reviewed?				

Checklist during the event

	Yes	No	Action	Comments
Have all coaches given clear demonstrations and explanations of the activities?				
Are all participants aware of the emergency procedures?				
Have all coaches adhered to the coaches responsibilities and emergency accident procedures?				
Injuries reported:				
Type:				
Have any near misses or serious injuries taken place?	Eg equipment failure. Eg misuse of equipment			

Post-event checklist

	Yes	No	Action	Comments
Were the overall health and safety procedures adhered to and understood during the event?				
Were all injuries reported and dealt with using the correct protocol?				
Did all external organisations cooperate effectively (eg local leisure centre, governing bodies, police etc)?				

This section focuses on P1, M1, P2, M2, D1, P3, M3 and D2.

Unit overview

The major goal of any sports coach is to maximise the potential of the individuals or performers, enabling athletes to achieve levels of performance to a degree that may not have been possible if left to their own endeavours.

The role of the coach can be complex and involved, yet exciting and rewarding. At any one time the coaches fulfil the role of instructor, assessor, friend, mentor, facilitator, demonstrator, advisor, supporter, fact finder, motivator, counsellor, organiser, planner and the 'fount of all knowledge'.

This unit allows you to develop your own knowledge of coaching by investigating the work of recognised successful coaches and reflecting on the reasons and means of their success. From here it is possible to move on and examine the tools of the trade, the techniques and strategies that successful coaches apply and the knowledge base needed to improve performance.

Learning outcomes

1 Understand the roles, responsibilities and skills of sports coaches (Grading criteria P1, P2, M1, M2, D1)

2 Understand the techniques used by coaches to improve the performance of athletes (Grading criteria P3, M3, D2)

These Learning Outcomes cover the roles, responsibilities and skills of sports coaches, and understanding the techniques used by coaches to improve the performance of athletes. We're not going to move on to planning and delivering a sports coaching session (Learning Outcomes 3 and 4) in this short book.

Content

1) **Understand the roles, responsibilities and skills of sports coaches**

   Roles: eg innovator, friend, manager, trainer, role-model, educator

   Responsibilities: eg legal obligations (child protection, insurance), professional conduct, health and safety, equal opportunities, knowledge of the coaching environment

   Skills: eg communication, organisation, analysing, problem solving, evaluating, time management.

2) **Understand the techniques used by coaches to improve the performance of athletes**

   Techniques: eg observation analysis, performance profiling, fitness assessment, goal setting simulation, modelling, effective demonstration, technical instruction, developing performer coaching diaries, adapting practices to meet individual needs, designing effective practice sessions.

Grading criteria

P1 describe four roles and four responsibilities of sports coaches, using examples of coaches from different sports

To achieve this grade you could consider two coaches from two different sports, one of which may be your own coach, and describe four roles and four responsibilities that each of these coaches possess. It would be a good idea to think of coaches from contrasting sports as this may help you as you progress through the grading criteria. For example a coach from a team sport, a coach from an individual sport, an international team coach or a coach from your local club.

To describe you need to paint a picture in words to make it easy to understand, as though the people reading this are new to coaching.

M1 explain four roles and four responsibilities of sports coaches, using examples of coaches from different sports

To achieve M1 you need to provide more depth by explaining four roles and four responsibilities of sports coaches. For this you could use the same coaches identified in P1, but to provide more detailed explanations of the roles and responsibilities you should use examples from case studies demonstrating how these roles and responsibilities have been applied.

To explain you need to imagine that the people reading this have little understanding of coaching, so you need to use clear examples of how the roles and responsibilities are used within different sports by the coaches.

P2 describe three skills common to successful sports coaches, using examples of coaches from different sports

To achieve P2 you could use the same coaches identified in P1 and M1. Looking at these coaches, describe three skills which they have in common in their success.

Remember you are describing, so paint that picture again! Make it easy to understand, describe why these skills are important.

M2 explain three skills common to successful sports coaches, using examples of coaches from different sports

M2 is an extension of P2 so requires more depth. To provide more detail in your explanation you need to use examples of how the coaches applied these skills in real situations, showing evidence of their success. For example, Liverpool Manager, Rafa Benitez, demonstrated good communication, problem solving and tactical organisational skills in the 2005 Champions League final after going 3 – 0 down to AC Milan to eventually draw 3 – 3 and then win on penalties.

D1 compare and contrast the roles, responsibilities and skills of successful coaches from different sports

To achieve D1 you are going to be looking at all the work you have done so far in P1, P2, M1 and M2. This requires a more analytical approach. You need to compare and contrast your coaches by looking at their similarities and differences within the roles, responsibilities and skills. For example, you may have identified the same roles but how do the coaches differ in the way they perform their roles? Are there differences because the sports are contrasting?

Are there differences because the coaches are contrasting?

For example, Alex Ferguson may find it easier as a motivator as he is dealing with elite, professional athletes. Graham Simm, an under 8's rugby coach, may find it harder to motivate his junior jaguar rugby team as they may have lower concentration levels and find it harder to remain focused. Analysing involves you identifying the key factors, and saying how they relate to the topic.

P3 describe three different techniques that are used, by coaches, to improve the performance of athletes

Select three different coaching techniques that are used by coaches and describe how these are used. Once again you should be describing these techniques as though somebody is reading about these for the first time. It should be clear and simple to understand. Using protocols and procedures of the techniques you select will help with your descriptions.

M3 explain three different techniques that are used by coaches to improve performance of athletes

To explain the three different techniques and achieve M3 you need more depth to the piece of work. To do this you could use case studies and explain how certain coaches have applied these techniques in their field to help improve performance of the athletes. For example, the fitness assessments used by Dave Reddin, the England Rugby Union team conditioner, before going on to win the 2003 World Cup.

D2 evaluate three different techniques that are used by coaches to improve the performance of athletes

To evaluate the three different techniques you need to look at results and how the techniques influenced the results, whether it is positive or negative. You could use case studies looking at how coaches have used different techniques in the run up to major championships and finals and evaluate these against the results. For example, Kelly Holmes' coach before winning double Olympic gold in Athens 2004. What goals did Kelly have in the run up to winning gold? Did she achieve these goals? Did goals change at any stage? Did they improve her performance?

Activities

In this section there will be a number of activities for you to complete. These will help you understand what you need to do to successfully achieve the grading criteria for learning outcomes 1 and 2.

Activities 1 to 13 cover P1, M1, D1

Activities 13 to 17 cover P2, M2, D1

Activities 18 and 19 cover P3, M3, D2

Learning outcome 1

1) Understanding the roles of sports coaches

For a coach to be effective and improve or promote change in a person's ability he or she will need to perform a number of different roles when coaching. These roles are varied and contrasting, with each one playing a significant role in developing the performer. A quality and conscientious coach, whether it be Steve McClaren with the England Football team or Dave Wilson with Hull Ionians Rugby Union 2nd team, they should pay equal amounts of attention to each role to be successful.

In this section you are going to take part in a number of activities that will help you identify and gain an understanding of the roles of a coach.

ACTIVITY 1

In small groups, choose a coach that you are familiar with. This could be a top professional coach or your own coach. Discuss and consider the different roles you think the coach has to perform and write them on the spider diagram. When you have completed the diagram, compare the roles you have identified with the other groups in your class.

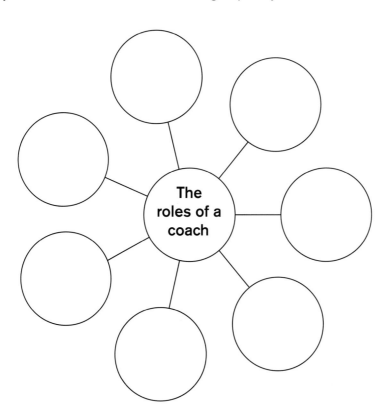

The roles of a coach

ACTIVITY 2

Now that you have identified the roles of a coach, you need to look at what is involved in these roles for different coaches in different sports.

Copy the table below. In pairs, discuss and write down your definition of each of the roles in the table. When you have completed this, use a dictionary to fill in the definitions next to yours and see how close you got.

Roles	Your definition	Dictionary definition
Manager		
Educator		
Trainer		
Role model		
Innovator		
Friend		
Motivator		

ACTIVITY 3

THE COACH AS A MANAGER

The case study across the page provides an insight into the weekly duties of a football manager. It demonstrates how much work goes into managing an elite football club – it does not just involve standing on a pitch side taking training mid week and match days.

Read the study carefully and write down eight different management tasks that take place week in week out during the football season.

Case study

It's a busy week for Tony Storr, the manager of Riverbank Athletic professional football club. Arriving at the training ground at 7.30 am on Monday morning, Tony sits down with his coaching team to plan the week's coaching, identifying the team and individual goals for the forthcoming week. After a poor performance the previous Saturday Tony reviewed the game on the Sunday and identified the areas where the team needs to improve. At 10 am a full team meeting takes place so the players can review the game and air their views, followed by a tough training session with the specialist coaches to begin correcting the problems.

While this takes place Tony sets about his administration duties and organises some alternative training venues for the week to help keep the coaching environment fresh and to keep the players motivated.

The end to a busy Monday sees Tony meet with the chairman for his weekly review, where he discusses team performance and looks at the financial strategies to help improve the squad. Managing the transfer budget as well as present players' contracts that are up for renewal are top of this agenda.

Tuesday: time for Tony to have his weekly one on ones with his squad, helping them identify areas for improvement as well as airing any personal issues so these can be addressed and help keep the player happy and motivated.

The rest of the week you will mainly find Tony at the training group overseeing the coaching and closely observing the players with an eye on team selection, which takes place on Thursday for Saturday's match.

ACTIVITY 4

THE ROLE AS AN INNOVATOR

Innovation is all about devising new ideas that will help with an athlete's development: keeping things fresh, preventing the sessions becoming stale and boring but ultimately helping progression and improved results. If coaching methods and ideas do not progress, the athlete has little chance of improving.

Research task

For this task you are to select two sports of your choice and using the internet and books identify a piece of innovative skill or technique that has changed the sport by improving results and performance.

Present your findings to the group, identifying:

- The skill or technique
- When it was first introduced
- Who introduced it
- How it made an impact on the sport.

ACTIVITY 5

THE ROLE OF MOTIVATOR

A major role in any success is motivation. If you are not motivated you will fail. If the coach manages the coaching environment effectively, understands the athlete as a person and what 'makes them tick', the athlete will be happy and motivated.

There are many factors that motivate people to take part in sport. Take five minutes to think and write down as many reasons as you can think of why people participate in sport.

As a class, collect all of your findings on a flip chart and then write down your own top three reasons for participating in sport.

Your top three reasons would help a coach to identify what would motivate you and help them to manage a coaching environment to suit you.

ACTIVITY 6

THE ROLE OF EDUCATOR

The principal aim of the coach as an educator is to teach skills and techniques in the chosen sport and provide the knowledge of how and when to apply these skills when taking part in their sport. With performers having different levels of ability and levels of learning, the coach needs to adapt their teaching style and methods to suit the performer.

As well as teaching skills and techniques, the coach is responsible for lifestyle education. Helping the athlete with areas such as emotional control, working as a team, fair play, citizenship, equality, communication, professionalism and the development of self-esteem.

Task 1

Who is the best coach you have ever had? Describe the best piece of skill or single technique they taught you. How old were you? What did they teach you? What did they say? Why did it influence you so much? Did it improve your performance?

Task 2

In small groups, select a sport and provide examples of when and how the lifestyle education factors have been demonstrated.

ACTIVITY 7

THE COACH AS A TRAINER

Even if the elite performer is the most technically gifted athlete in the world, if they are not physically conditioned for the specific demands of their sport they will not perform to their optimum level.

Read the case study below, which looks at how the England Rugby team prepare for the physical demands of their sport, and then complete Tasks 1 – 3.

Case study

For any sports performer, preparation can never be overlooked, including for the world rugby union champions, England. Since the move towards professional status, the Rugby Football Union has employed many professional coaches to ensure that players have the best support for technical and physical development.

In modern sport physical conditioning has become more evident. Even those positions in rugby that – in the past – have favoured larger-framed players who may not have been as physically conditioned are finding the pace of the new 'modern game' just too fast without such physical conditioning.

A variety of training methods is used to ensure that players are prepared; these can include sprinting drills, free-weight sessions, and endurance conditioning. Often the main body of physical conditioning starts in the pre-season of a rugby campaign and the conditioning coach will work each component of physical fitness as appropriate for each player and their position. Then, as the season begins, the conditioning coach objective will be to maintain the levels of fitness of the players and to work around injuries and areas of fitness that may require attention throughout the season.

Task 1

Observe a warm-up of an international rugby game; observe what preparation the rugby teams undertake and the role of the coach in this preparation.

Task 2

a) Observe a conditioning session led by a professional sports conditioner. Describe the roles played by the conditioner in the training session and explain the methods of communication used by the conditioner when communicating to the athletes and delivering the training methods.

b) For each method of training, identify the components of fitness that are being targeted.

Task 3

Name the components of fitness that are required to be an international centre? And an international prop forward? Place the components in order of importance for these specific roles.

ACTIVITY 8

THE COACH AS A ROLE MODEL

Coaches can be very influential people and it is often said that performers reflect the coach's attitudes and attributes. A coach needs to set a high standard in professionalism and have the trust of their athletes at all times. These qualities will help the coach succeed in being a positive role model.

You may or may not have realised, but at some stage in your life you will have had a role model who has influenced you in your actions.

There is no set format for a relationship with a role model, it could be a school teacher, a coach, somebody who offers you advice or possibly somebody you look up to in the world of professional sport or business.

Think of somebody who has had a positive influence on you in your life, this could be in any area not just sport, and describe the influences he/she had on you.

2) Understanding the responsibilities of sports coaches

The coach has a responsibility to develop the sports performer in his or her chosen sport to the best of their ability in a professional, safe and ethical environment, delivering the appropriate level of coaching for the performer's needs.

For the coach to achieve success in a professional coaching environment they must fulfil a number of responsibilities that will set a good example, providing an excellent learning environment for the performer and in so doing helping the coach become a good role model.

ACTIVITY 9

In small groups select a sports coach of your choice. This can be a professional coach or your own local club coach. Discuss what responsibilities the coach has and write your answers into a spider diagram like the one on the right:

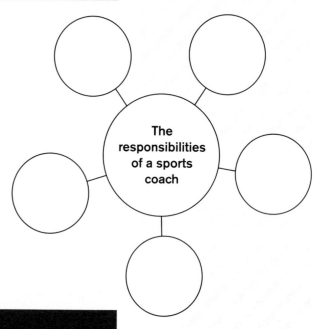

ACTIVITY 10

COACHING ENVIRONMENT RESPONSIBILITIES

Responsibilities and aims in the coaching environment can be wide and varied: from a tennis beginner being able to hit a forehand correctly to achieving high levels of success on the international stage with an elite athlete. Coaching sessions should have a specific aim to meet and improve the level of ability, whether it is tennis player Roger Federer or Andy Forth, a club table tennis player. Every session should be well planned and organised, demonstrate progression and maximise the potential of the performer. It is important that the coach provides a rewarding and enjoyable environment to keep the performer motivated. This will be key to achieving results.

Case study

Dave is an FA level 1 football coach and coaches an under 14 boys' football team. The team finished mid-table and have reached the final of the league cup after finishing near the bottom of the league the previous season. They train three times a week for two hours with a fitness session on a Monday, skills on a Wednesday and match tactics and drills on a Thursday. The sessions are well attended with 20 players there every week. The players are the same as the previous season. The captain, Pete, has been selected to represent the county team for the first time and has played five games this season with one game to go. The game falls on the same day as the cup final and Dave says the final should be his priority as he is the captain, the best player, and not playing could demotivate the team. Feeling under pressure Pete decides to play in the final so not to let his team mates down.

Dave has already signed eight new players for next season, but has decided not to start up a second team as he believes competition for places will help improve performance, which will result in progression and promotion.

During the off season Dave will begin his FA level 2 qualification and a treatment of injuries course.

Split the class into two groups and read the case study above. Group one will present the positive points from the case study, highlighting what areas the coach has got right in the coaching environment.

Group two is to present the negative aspects of the case study.

Finally, as a full group discuss what could have been done differently.

ACTIVITY 11

HEALTH AND SAFETY RESPONSIBILITIES (LINKS TO UNIT 2, LEARNING OUTCOME 4)

Health and safety is an essential element in the coaching environment. Risks should be minimised before and during the session, with the performer's welfare at the forefront of the coach's thoughts.

The three main areas of health and safety that are the responsibility of the coach are:

1) The safety of the facilities
2) The safety of the activities
3) The safety of the participants.

Facilities – The coach is responsible for producing a full risk assessment of the facility before the session takes place, to help them deal with any given situation that may arise and to highlight, and correct, risk factors before the session begins.

Task 1

In small groups, research different types of risk assessment forms. Following this produce an appropriate risk assessment form for a sports facility used on your course and complete the assessment, presenting your findings to the group.

Activities: the coach should select activities which the performer is physically capable of achieving and use professional practice to prevent risk to the athlete. The correct protocols, procedures and techniques should be used at all times. Key areas are:

- warm-up
- cool-down
- activities coached within the rules and regulations of the sport
- technically correct coaching methods applied
- activities meet performers physical and technical capabilities.

Task 2

Select a sport of your choice and design a ten-minute warm-up for an elite performer/s in that sport, which follows all health and safety guidelines.

Participant – The key areas that will ensure the safety of the participant are addressing the safety of the facilities and equipment, and making sure the correct activities are coached. The coach needs to adhere to the good practice guidelines within their sport.

ACTIVITY 12

PROFESSIONAL CONDUCT RESPONSIBILITIES

A coach can be seen as being 'a leader' in their sport, which leads to a position of influence, power and responsibility. A coach needs to have the knowledge of how to use this position without abusing it. All coaches' actions should reflect good practice and appropriate behaviour that is professional, fair, honest, competent and considerate to the individual performer's needs.

In small groups, select a sport and through research produce a poster in your sport highlighting the professional codes of conduct, with an example of how these have been performed in a positive way and in a negative way.

ACTIVITY 13

LEGAL RESPONSIBILITIES

Coaches need to be fully aware of their legal obligations. Although they have obligations within the rules and regulations of their sport, coaches are like any other citizen bound by the laws of the land. They must have the knowledge of how the law affects their coaching and the athletes under their supervision.

Below is a table identifying five Acts that a coach must take into consideration and abide by. Give a brief example of how these Acts could affect a coach's work.

Act	Effect
Disability Discrimination Act	
Race Relations Act	
Childrens Act	
Equal Opportunities Act	
Occupiers' Liability Act	

3) Understanding the skills of sports coaches

For a coach to be successful at any level, whether it is elite or beginner, they need to possess a wide range of skills and have the confidence to express them within their field. These skills are found in everyday life and are not exclusive to sports coaching. While studying for your National Diploma you should be demonstrating these skills, week in week out.

ACTIVITY 14

In pairs, discuss and identify the skills required to be a successful sports coach. To help, you could think about the everyday skills that you use and need to complete your studies. Make a chart like the one below.

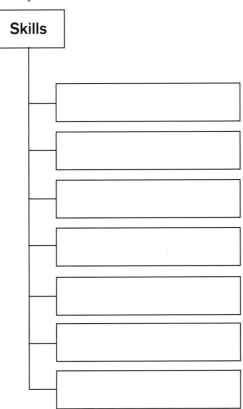

ACTIVITY 15

VERBAL AND NON-VERBAL COMMUNICATION

Communication is about the sharing of meaningful information successfully through knowledge and experiences between coach and athlete.

A successful coach will demonstrate good communication skills and in doing so will achieve results. It is important that the coach understands that communication is a two-way process. There are the coach's signals in the form of verbal and non-verbal communication, and the receiving of a signal, listening and understanding. The athletes' signals are as important as the coach's, as the coach has to determine actions with the help gained from the signals they receive.

Task 1

As a group, discuss the characteristics that make up verbal and non-verbal communication. When you have agreed these, write them on a flip chart.

Each member of the group should give an example of how one of these characteristics has been expressed in professional sport.

Task 2

Listening and understanding

It is important that the coach and athlete go through the process of listening, hearing, understanding and accepting.

Give an example of when this process has been successful with a positive result, and an example of when the process has broken down and culminated in a negative result.

ACTIVITY 16

ORGANISATIONAL SKILLS

For a coach to deliver an effective coaching session in their field they must have good organisational skills. Effective organisation is made up of a number of skills, which if addressed properly will culminate in a well-delivered session.

The word 'organise' can have a broad meaning in the world of sports coaching. One form of organisation could be the planning of sessions, making sure that everything is ready and prepared to help deliver a smooth and effective session meeting aims and objectives.

Analysing and problem solving also require a high degree of organisational skills, as these are constantly tested in the field, correcting or changing people's actions while instructing, or changing their actions for tactical reasons in a competition. Finally a coach has to be organised in their administration duties.

A local sports centre manager has asked you to organise a two-hour sports afternoon.

In pairs, write down everything you need to know and do before the session to make it as organised and effective as possible.

ACTIVITY 17

ANALYSING AND PROBLEM SOLVING

A major part of a coach's job is about analysing performers' actions, measuring the performance against goals and addressing the coaching practices to meet the desired level of performance and/or improve it.

Problems will occur within the coaching process and this provides the coach with their biggest, yet possibly most rewarding challenge.

Below are four areas where possible problems may occur.

The performer	The coaching environment	The competitive arena	The coach

Divide into four groups, with each group being allocated one area. Discuss your area and the problems that may occur and present one example to the other groups, stating the problem encountered and how it could be overcome. Answers page 27

Now as a class, think about situations that have occurred in professional sport and how these problems have been overcome.

LEARNING OUTCOME 2

2) Understanding techniques used by sports coaches to improve performance

There are many techniques that can be used to teach a performer a new skill and to improve performance. Each has its own merits and has proved effective within the coaching process. A particular technique which is used by a coach will depend on a number of factors. For example, the skill to be taught, the performer's needs and aspirations, the performer's ability and skill level, the coaching environment and the level of qualification of the coach, to name a few. In this section we are going to look at three different coaching techniques and identify how and when they might be applied.

ACTIVITY 18

Below is a table identifying three different techniques used to improve an athlete's performance.

Research the techniques and the procedures of how the techniques are performed. Then think of an example of how this could be used in a sport of your choice to improve performance. Copy the table below, and write your procedures and examples in your table.

Technique	Procedures	Example
Fitness assessments Multi-stage fitness – bleep test		
Illinois agility run		
Notational/video analysis		
Goal setting		

ACTIVITY 19

Split the class into three groups and allocate one of the three coaching techniques to each group.

As a group, select a professional athlete of your choice. Each group must have an athlete from a contrasting sport. Devise a timeline of the athlete's career highlighting their achievements, and present to the class an evaluation of how the identified techniques would have been used and improved the performance of the athletes.

ANSWERS

ACTIVITY 1

Here are the main roles of a coach, which are the same whether you chose a club coach or an elite performance coach. All coaches should have these roles at the forefront of their minds.

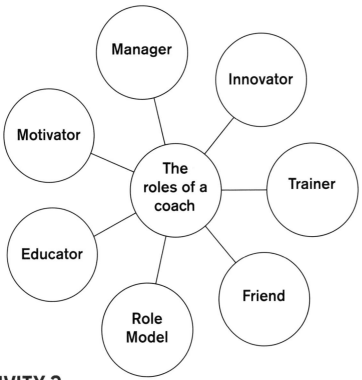

ACTIVITY 3

1) Managing the coaching environment
2) Man management
3) Team selection
4) Organising coaching staff to develop performers
5) Manage and plan the coaching programmes
6) Administration – registration of players, travel, organising venues etc
7) Financial management
8) Performance management.

ACTIVITY 5

Some of the reasons for taking part in sport:

- Enjoyment
- Meet people
- Challenge themselves
- Improve fitness
- The competitive environment
- Improve performance
- To win
- To please others.

ACTIVITY 9

The chart below provides the five main responsibilities of a coach. How many did you get right from your discussion?

ACTIVITY 11

1) The safety of the *facilities*

2) The safety of the *activities*

3) The safety of the *participants*.

ACTIVITY 14

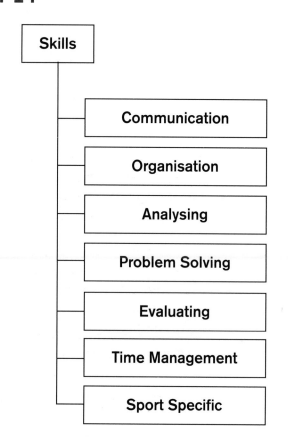

ACTIVITY 15

Verbal communication: speaking, varying the volume, varying the pace, varying the tone

Non-verbal communication: body language, facial expressions – smiles, frowns, eye movements, laughter – and gestures.

ACTIVITY 17

The performer: unable to carry out a skill

The coaching environment: double booking for facilities or bad weather

The competitive arena: difficulty with opponent or team requiring tactical changes

The coach: performer unable to understand due to poor communication.

This section focuses on grading criteria P1, P2, P3; M1 and M2; D1.

Unit overview

Psychology for sports performance is the search for understanding how psychological factors and issues affect sports performance. Throughout this unit you will appreciate how the sports performer is affected by their personality and motivation. The unit will also explore the close relationship between arousal, stress and anxiety and their effects on sports performance.

Key topics are what make a sports performer unique, including the psychological core, typical responses and sports behaviour. An understanding of each of these issues is imperative in getting the best from your athlete.

The effects on sports performance from arousal, stress and anxiety will be examined and explained, including both the negative and positive psychological and physiological responses. In practice, if a sports performer can control these factors, optimal performance can be achieved.

From this unit information, the effects of each factor can be examined and applied to sports performance.

Learning outcomes

1 Understand the effects of personality and motivation on sports performance
2 Understand the relationships between stress, anxiety, arousal and sports performance.

Content

1) **Understand the effects of personality and motivation on sports performance**

Personality: definition; theories (trait theories, social learning theory, situational approach, interactional approach, type A, type B); types (type A, type B); effects on sports performance (athletes versus non-athletes, individual versus team sports, elite versus non-elite athletes, type A versus type B)

Motivation: definition; types (intrinsic, extrinsic, achievement motivation); theories,

eg attribution theory; effects on sports performance (positive, negative, future expectations of success and failure).

2) **Understand the relationships between stress, anxiety, arousal and sports performance**

Stress: definition; types (eustress and distress); causes (internal, external, personal, occupational, sports environments); cognitive, somatic and behavioural effects of stress (effects of activating the sympathetic and parasympathetic nervous systems)

Anxiety: definition; types (state and trait anxiety, cognitive and somatic symptoms of stress); effects on sports performance (negative mental state, loss of self confidence and decreased expectations of success, fear of failure)

Arousal: definition; theories (drive theory, inverted U hypothesis, catastrophe theory, individual zones of optimal functioning); effects on sports performance (improvements and decrements in performance level, changes in attention focus, increases in anxiety levels, choking).

Grading criteria

P1 describe personality and how it affects sports performance

For this criterion you must be able to describe personality and then how personality affects sports performance. The description must include a definition, personality theories, personality types and effects on sports performance

P2 describe motivation and how it affects sports performance

For P2 you must describe the factors that affect motivation of athletes. You must include a definition of motivation, types of motivation and the effects of motivation on sports performance

P3 describe stress, anxiety and arousal, their causes and their effects on sports performance

To meet grading criterion P3 you must describe stress, anxiety and arousal, their causes and how they affect sports performance; the description must include definitions and also list types of stress and anxiety and theories of arousal

M1 explain the effects of personality and motivation on sports performance

Grading criterion M1 is an extension of grading criteria P1 and P2, requiring you to explain the effects of personality and motivation on sports performance in greater depth with reference to theories of motivation, including need achievement, attribution and achievement motivation

M2 explain the effects of stress, anxiety and arousal on sports performance

For grading criterion M2, which builds upon grading criterion P3, you must explain the effects of stress, anxiety and arousal on

sports performance in greater detail. You will be required to explain physiological and psychological symptoms, including sources of stress and anxiety and arousal. You will also include how stress, arousal and anxiety affect performance, drive theory, inverted U hypothesis, catastrophe theory, zones of optimal functioning, are all related to sports performance

D1 evaluate the effects of personality and motivation on sports performance

Grading criterion D1 is a further extension of grading criterion M1, which requires you to evaluate the effects of personality and motivation on sports performance. This means you must make a judgement based on each of the effects that you have described/explained (grading criteria P1, P2 and M1). This will evaluate personality and behaviour.

LEARNING OUTCOME 1

1) Understand the effects of personality and motivation on sports performance

In this section we will focus on grading criteria P1, P2, M1 and D1 from Unit 16 – Psychology for Sports Performance.

ACTIVITY 1

WHAT MAKES UP OUR PERSONALITY?

Make a table like the one below. Using the example inserted within the table, decide on what your behaviour in each of the situations/environments would be. Describe how you would act in each section.

On your own	In the classroom		On the sports field		With friends out of
Quiet	Shy	Aggressive	Outgoing	Lethargic	Loud

Compare your answers with another member of the class. Discuss the differences, if any, at each situation.

ACTIVITY 2

Research and define the following terminology:

- Psychological core
- Typical responses
- Role-related behaviours.

Create a table like the one below, and insert your details to summarise your research.

Psychological core	
Typical responses	
Role-related	

Use your findings from the task to indicate on the triangle where each of the terms is located.

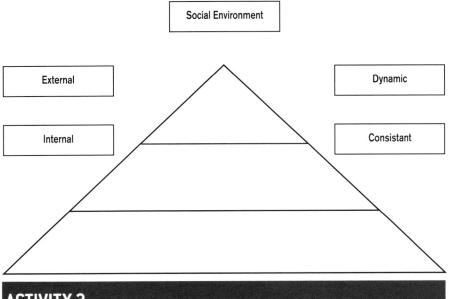

Social Environment

External

Dynamic

Internal

Consistant

ACTIVITY 3

Conduct an experiment into personality types with yourself and your partner.

The experiment

Equipment:
- Lemon juice
- Kitchen scales
- Cotton wool balls

Experimental protocol:
- Put a large drop of lemon juice on your tongue and swill it around your mouth for ten seconds
- Use the cotton wool balls to mop up all the saliva that you produce
- When you've mopped it all up, put the cotton wool balls on your kitchen scales and see how much they weigh
- Compare your results with yourself and your partner, and see whose cotton ball weighs the most.

Discussion:
- With your partner, try and account for the differences in weight due to differences in personality. Use key psychological rather than physiological terminology.

Expected results:
- That introverts produce a lot of saliva in response to lemon juice
- That extroverts don't produce much saliva in response to lemon juice.

(adapted from www.bbc.co.uk)

ACTIVITY 4

Read the following description of trait theories.

Psychologists consider the trait theory is a key issue when discussing approaches to personality. This theory assumes that all sports performers' personalities are relatively stable across environments and situations. Thus athletes are born with the traits that they possess and display. For example, a sports performer who is aggressive and competitive will always perform to their maximum, even if they are losing.

Esyenck suggested that traits could be grouped into two continuums:

Extroversion_____Introversion

Active	Inactive
Energetic	Lethargic
Social	Easily tied
Little concern for possible consequences	Self conscious
	Safety and security
Variety is the spice of life	Ruled by fears

Stable _____Neuroticism or emotionality

Emotionally stable people have good emotional control	Neuroticism or emotionality is characterised by high levels of negative effect
Experience negative effect only in the face of very major stresses	Depression and anxiety
Calm and collected under pressure	Fight-or-flight response in the face of danger

Using the trait approach, copy the diagram below. Place the listed athletes where you think they may be located.

- Yourself
- David Beckham
- Paula Radcliffe
- Wayne Rooney
- Sven-Göran Eriksson
- Steve Redgrave
- Jonny Wilkinson
- Amir Khan
- Tim Henman
- Andrew Flintoff
- Tiger Woods
- Paul Cooke
- Mike Tyson

ACTIVITY 5

SOCIAL LEARNING THEORY

This theory suggests that when a sports performer's behaviour is reinforced through positive feedback, the behaviour is likely to be repeated.

Case study

An Under 16s rugby league player has been watching the Super League Play Offs on television; the young athlete notices that when Team A are tackling Team B, they are being very aggressive in the tackle, trash talking the opposition, giving their opposing players a facial by rubbing their hands in the opposition faces. Team A goes unpunished. The young athlete decides to use his role model's behaviour in his next fixture, his behaviour is then positively reinforced by his own coach.

Using this scenario, can you identify any problems or issues with Social Learning Theory?

ACTIVITY 6

SITUATIONAL APPROACH

This theory suggests that the environment influences a sports performer's behaviour.

For example, aggression is needed on the field in many contact sports, but off the field the sports performer is introverted and non-aggressive.

Can you identify any sports performers where aggression is encouraged on the field, ie personality is influenced by the environment? Make a table like the one below, and fill in your responses.

Sports performer	Influence on behaviour

ACTIVITY 7

INTERACTIONAL APPROACH

This theory considers that both the situation and the person determine behaviour. Therefore both the personality of the sports performer and the environment will play an important role in understanding an athlete's behaviour.

Scenario

You are the coach of a Boot Camp Exercise Circuit Class. Each week your athletes take it in turn to design and lead the exercises within your class. You have two new athletes to your class; however, you have coached them from an early age, and have been able to determine their personalities.

Athlete A, is confident, has high levels of self esteem and displays natural leadership qualities.

Athlete B, is nervous when meeting new people, self conscious and has low self esteem.

Working in small groups, identify which athlete will drop out of the exercise circuit class.

Explain why this athlete has dropped out of the exercise circuit class.

Identify strategies that could be used to increase the participation rates from your athlete that has dropped out.

ACTIVITY 8

TYPE A AND TYPE B PERSONALITY THEORY

On the opposite page is a list of statements related to everyday living.

Indicate on a scale of 1–5 the degree to which each applies to you.

(Scale value 1 – never, 2 – rarely, 3 – sometimes, 4 – frequently, 5 – always)

	Score
1 I want to be the best at everything I do	
2 I get annoyed in traffic jams	
3 I become impatient when waiting in line	
4 I find myself getting angry if kept waiting for an appointment	
5 I like to drive my car very fast	
6 I get angry with co-workers who are inefficient	
7 I find I try harder than others to accomplish things	
8 I seem to put more effort into my job than other people	
9 I get irritable when others don't take their job seriously	
10 I am determined to win when playing a game with friends	
11 I enjoy intense competition	
12 When playing a game with a child, I will purposely let him or her win	
13 I move, walk, talk and eat rapidly	
14 I feel impatient because most things happen too slowly	
15 I think about school work constantly	
16 I feel guilty when I relax and take it easy	
17 I challenge people about their thoughts and ideas	
18 I seem to have little spare time	
19 I do my work faster and more efficiently that others	
20 I enjoy discussing my achievement	
21 I become angry, easily, with male or female friends	
22 I find that I am quiet or subdued	
23 I appear more aggressive than others	
24 I let others know when I am angry	
25 I find I have insufficient time to finish my work	
26 I become confused when too many things happen at once	
27 I wish I had help to get things done	
28 I rely only on myself to get things done	
29 Relaxing seems to infringe on my work time	
30 I skip meals to get things done	
31 I do extra work to impress others	
32 I seem to race against the clock to save time	
33 I lose my temper under pressure	
34 I make mistakes because I feel rushed into things without thinking them through completely	

The average score is 102.

Values under 80 are considered to belong to Type B personality.

Values of 80 or above are considered to belong to Type A personality.

Scores between 0–29 equal a Type B personality; you are relaxed and cope well with stress.

Scores between 30–59 equal a Type B personality; you are generally relaxed and cope adequately with stress.

Scores between 60–79 equal a Type A/B personality; you are a mixture of both types, which is healthy.

Scores between 80–109 equal a Type A personality; you do not cope well with stress and are prone to developing stress.

Scores between 110–140 equal a Type A personality; you are extremely likely to suffer from stress.

How did you do?

ACTIVITY 9

EFFECTS ON SPORTS PERFORMANCE

In psychological terms, do elite athletes and non-elite athletes differ in personality traits?

Conduct an experiment into personality types with yourself and your partner.

The experiment

Equipment:

- Questionnaire.

Experimental protocol:

- Conduct the questionnaire with ten elite athletes
- Conduct the questionnaire with ten non-elite athletes
- Plot your data on the template below.

Discussion:

- Discuss the results with your partner. Try to explain the differences between elite athletes and non-elite athletes and your results
- How do your results compare with the graph of Successful Elite Athletes and Unsuccessful Non-Elite Athletes?

Psychological profile assessment

On the opposite page is a list of words that describe feelings that people experience. Ask your elite athletes and non-elite athletes to read each one carefully. Then circle ONE number to the right, which best describes HOW THEY FEEL IN GENERAL.

MAKE SURE THEY HAVE ANSWERED EVERY ITEM.

0 = Not at all

1 = A little

2 = Moderately

3 = Quite a bit

4 = Extremely

1 Friendly	0 1 2 3 4	34 Nervous	0 1 2 3 4
2 Tense	0 1 2 3 4	35 Lonely	0 1 2 3 4
3 Angry	0 1 2 3 4	36 Miserable	0 1 2 3 4
4 Worn out	0 1 2 3 4	37 Muddled	0 1 2 3 4
5 Unhappy	0 1 2 3 4	38 Cheerful	0 1 2 3 4
6 Clear-headed	0 1 2 3 4	39 Bitter	0 1 2 3 4
7 Lively	0 1 2 3 4	40 Exhausted	0 1 2 3 4
8 Confused	0 1 2 3 4	41 Anxious	0 1 2 3 4
9 Sorry for things done	0 1 2 3 4	42 Ready to fight	0 1 2 3 4
10 Shaky	0 1 2 3 4	43 Good natured	0 1 2 3 4
11 Listless	0 1 2 3 4	44 Gloomy	0 1 2 3 4
12 Peeved	0 1 2 3 4	45 Desperate	0 1 2 3 4
13 Considerate	0 1 2 3 4	46 Sluggish	0 1 2 3 4
14 Sad	0 1 2 3 4	47 Rebellious	0 1 2 3 4
15 Active	0 1 2 3 4	48 Helpless	0 1 2 3 4
16 On edge	0 1 2 3 4	49 Weary	0 1 2 3 4
17 Grouchy	0 1 2 3 4	50 Bewildered	0 1 2 3 4
18 Blue	0 1 2 3 4	51 Alert	0 1 2 3 4
19 Energetic	0 1 2 3 4	52 Deceived	0 1 2 3 4
20 Panicky	0 1 2 3 4	53 Furious	0 1 2 3 4
21 Hopeless	0 1 2 3 4	54 Efficient	0 1 2 3 4
22 Relaxed	0 1 2 3 4	55 Trusting	0 1 2 3 4
23 Unworthy	0 1 2 3 4	56 Full of pep	0 1 2 3 4
24 Spiteful	0 1 2 3 4	57 Bad-tempered	0 1 2 3 4
25 Sympathetic	0 1 2 3 4	58 Worthless	0 1 2 3 4
26 Uneasy	0 1 2 3 4	59 Forgetful	0 1 2 3 4
27 Restless	0 1 2 3 4	60 Carefree	0 1 2 3 4
28 Unable to concentrate	0 1 2 3 4	61 Terrified	0 1 2 3 4
29 Fatigued	0 1 2 3 4	62 Guilty	0 1 2 3 4
30 Helpful	0 1 2 3 4	63 Vigorous	0 1 2 3 4
31 Annoyed	0 1 2 3 4	64 Uncertain about things	0 1 2 3 4
32 Discouraged	0 1 2 3 4	65 Bushed	0 1 2 3 4
33 Resentful	0 1 2 3 4		

Add up the results for each factor and input into totals column.

Mood state	Question number	Totals
Tension	2,10,16,20,26,27,34,41	
Depression	5,9,14,18,21,23,32,35,36	
Anger	3,12,17,24,31,33,39,42,47,52,53,57	
Vigour	7,15,19,38,51,56,60	
Fatigue	4,11,29,40,46,49,65	
Confusion	8,28,37,50,59,64	

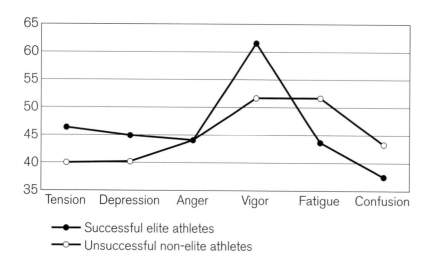

—●— Successful elite athletes
—○— Unsuccessful non-elite athletes

ACTIVITY 10

ATHLETE VERSUS NON-ATHLETE

Extroversion/introversion

Activity questionnaire

Conduct this questionnaire on an athlete and a non-athlete.

Scoring

Each question scores either one, half or zero points:

If you checked Yes* or No* (i.e. with an *) then allot one point.
If you checked Maybe then allot half a point.
If you checked Yes or No (i.e. without an *) then allot zero points.
Enter your score after each question, then add up the total for that trait.

Are you happiest when you get involved in some project that calls for immediate and rapid activity?
Yes* | Maybe | No || Score:

Do you become restless when working at something and little action is occurring?
Yes* | Maybe | No || Score:

When climbing stairs do you usually take them two at a time?
Yes* | Maybe | No || Score:

Are you inclined to be slow and deliberate in your actions?
Yes | Maybe | No* || Score:

Do you usually finish your meals before other people even though there is no reason to hurry?
Yes* | Maybe | No || Score:

Do other people regard you as a very lively person?
Yes* | Maybe | No || Score:

Are you always 'on the go' when not actually sleeping?
Yes* | Maybe | No || Score:

Do you like organising and initiating leisure activities?
Yes* | Maybe | No || Score:

When driving a car, do you get very frustrated by slow-moving traffic?
Yes* | Maybe | No || Score:

Are you generally very enthusiastic about starting a new project or undertaking?
Yes* | Maybe | No || Score:

When you are walking with other people, do they often have difficulty keeping up with you?
Yes* | Maybe | No || Score:

At work or at play, do other people find it hard to keep up with the pace you set?
Yes* | Maybe | No || Score:

Are you inclined to rush from one activity to another without pausing for rest?
Yes* | Maybe | No || Score:

Do you often find yourself hurrying to get to places, even when there is plenty of time?
Yes* | Maybe | No || Score:

Are you frequently lacking in energy and motivation to do things?
Yes | Maybe | No* || Score:

Do you like to lie in bed late at the weekends?
Yes | Maybe | No* || Score:

Do you prefer holidays that are quiet and restful without a great deal of rushing about?
Yes | Maybe | No* || Score:

Do you generally move about at a leisurely pace?
Yes | Maybe | No* || Score:

When you wake up in the morning are you usually ready to 'get cracking'?
Yes* | Maybe | No || Score:

Are you usually full of pep and vigour?
Yes* | Maybe | No || Score:

Do you often feel tired and listless?
Yes | Maybe | No* || Score:

Do you like to have a lot of things to do all the time?
Yes* | Maybe | No || Score:

Do other people seem to get more done in a day than you?
Yes | Maybe | No* || Score:

Most days, are there times when you enjoy just sitting and doing nothing?
Yes | Maybe | No* || Score:

Would you rather watch sports than play them?
Yes | Maybe | No* || Score:

Do you frequently take a nap in the middle of the day?
Yes | Maybe | No* || Score:

Do you get agitated if you have to wait for someone?
Yes* | Maybe | No || Score:

If you had to wait a few minutes for the lift, would you prefer to use the stairs instead?
Yes* | Maybe | No || Score:

Normally, do you tend to do things as quickly as you can?
Yes* | Maybe | No || Score:

Do you often feel bubbling over with excess energy?
Yes* | Maybe | No || Score:

Analysis

People scoring high on this trait are generally active and energetic, enjoying all kinds of physical activity including hard work and exercise, pursuing a wide variety of different interests.

People with low scores are inclined to be physically inactive, lethargic and easily tired. They prefer leisurely activities and find it hard to get going in the morning.

High activity is an extrovert characteristic: such people are outgoing because they have clear goals and knows what they want – this provides the energy. Low activity tends to go with introversion: a more inward-looking, self-conscious and inhibited personality. The person's goals may not be as clear – he or she may have suffered failure or trauma in the past and therefore have less confidence and energy.

The norm on this trait is 16–17 points.

How do your athlete and non-athlete scores compare?

Explain why personality affects sports performance.

ACTIVITY 11

INDIVIDUAL VERSUS TEAM SPORTS PERFORMERS

Activity questionnaire

Conduct this questionnaire on a team sports athlete and an individual sports athlete.

Scoring

Each question scores either one, half or zero points:

If you checked Yes* or No* (i.e. with an *) then allot one point.
If you checked Maybe then allot half a point.
If you checked Yes or No (i.e. without an *) then allot zero points.
Enter your score after each question, then add up the total for that trait.

Do you like going out a lot?
Yes* | Maybe | No || Score:

Do you often need understanding friends to cheer you up?
Yes* | Maybe | No || Score:

Generally, do you prefer reading to meeting people?
Yes | Maybe | No* || Score:

Are you fairly talkative when you are with a group of people?
Yes* | Maybe | No || Score:

Can you usually let yourself go and have a good time at a party?
Yes* | Maybe | No || Score:

Do you hate being with a crowd who play practical jokes on one another?
Yes | Maybe | No* || Score:

Do you like talking to people so much that you never miss a chance of talking to a stranger?
Yes* | Maybe | No || Score:

If you were making a business enquiry, would you rather write than discuss it on the telephone?
Yes | Maybe | No* || Score:

Do you enjoy spending long periods of time by yourself?
Yes | Maybe | No* || Score:

Are you relaxed and self confident in the company of other people?
Yes* | Maybe | No || Score:

Are you more distant and reserved than most people?
Yes | Maybe | No* || Score:

Do you like mixing with lots of other people?
Yes* | Maybe | No || Score:

Do you easily make new friends with members of your own sex?
Yes* | Maybe | No || Score:

Do you like to tell jokes and stories to groups of friends?
Yes* | Maybe | No || Score:

Do you enjoy talking and playing with young children?
Yes* | Maybe | No || Score:

Are you apprehensive about going into a room full of strange people?
Yes | Maybe | No* || Score:

Have you ever seriously felt that you might be happier living by yourself on a desert island?
Yes | Maybe | No* || Score:

Do you sometimes feel uncomfortable when people get close to you physically?
Yes | Maybe | No* || Score:

Is it important to you to be liked by a wide range of people?
Yes* | Maybe | No || Score:

Do you spontaneously introduce yourself to strangers at social gatherings?
Yes* | Maybe | No || Score:

Would you rather spend an evening talking to one interesting person of your own sex than being with a large crowd of friends?
Yes | Maybe | No* || Score:

Do you like to be in the middle of things?
Yes* | Maybe | No || Score:

Do you enjoy solitary activities such as reading or watching TV on your own?
Yes | Maybe | No* || Score:

Are you inclined to avoid people whenever possible?
Yes | Maybe | No* || Score:

Would you be unhappy if you were prevented from making numerous friends?
Yes* | Maybe | No || Score:

Do you usually prefer to be with companions than do things on your own?
Yes* | Maybe | No || Score:

Do you like to have a full calendar of engagements?
Yes* | Maybe | No || Score:

Are you inclined to limit your acquaintances to a select few?
Yes | Maybe | No* || Score:

Do you enjoy entertaining people?
Yes* | Maybe | No || Score:

Do you often feel ill at ease with other people?
Yes | Maybe | No* || Score:

Analysis

People scoring high on this trait tend to seek out the company of others, they like social functions such as parties and dances and are comfortable when meeting new people. They are extroverted and unselfconscious in company.

People with low scores prefer to have only a few special friends (who are like them) and most enjoy doing things on their own. They tend to be self-conscious and worry about finding things to talk about with other people. Though they may feel content enough, they seem to others to be introverted and, maybe, unfriendly. They have probably had frustrating or humiliating experiences in the past when trying to communicate and so they avoid risking a repetition. They may justify this with a consideration that others are unintelligent or trivial, further solidifying their inhibition. Or they may feel that they have better things to do!

The norm on this trait is 16–17 points.

How do your team sports athlete and an individual sports athlete scores compare?

Explain why personality affects sports participation.

ACTIVITY 12

MOTIVATION

Try to define motivation using some key words to aid your explanation.

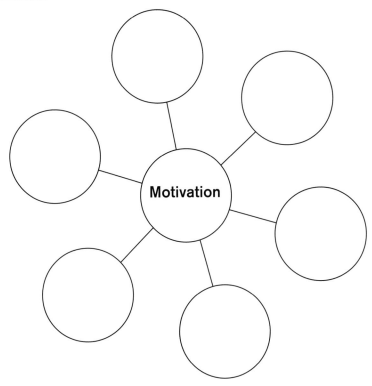

ACTIVITY 13

INTRINSIC, EXTRINSIC

Case study

Lee Briers at Warrington is an elite-level performer.

Lee Briers remaining at the club he was contracted to and refused to leave even though the money offered at other rugby league clubs was greater.

Rio Ferdinand is an elite-level performer.

Rio Ferdinand allegedly refused to sign a contract at Manchester United in July 2005. It was reported that Rio refused to sign a contract that was offered by the club until it matched his own valuation of £100 000 a week.

Create two diagrams like the one overleaf, and describe the forms of motivation for both elite-level sports performers.

Lee   **Rio**

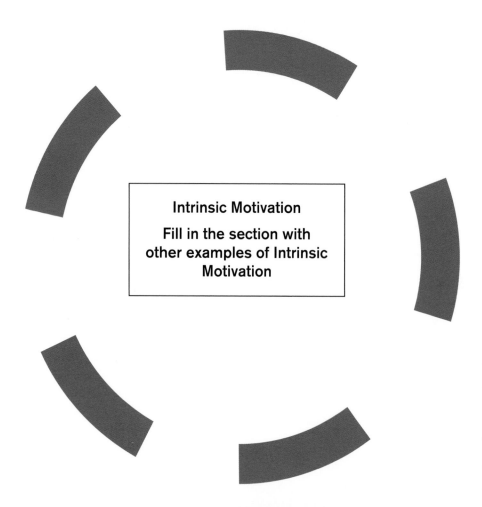

Intrinsic Motivation

Fill in the section with other examples of Intrinsic Motivation

ACTIVITY 14

ACHIEVEMENT MOTIVATION

This terminology is important in developing sports performance. To understand how achievement motivation improves sports performance, it is vital to appreciate the full meaning of achievement motivation. Achievement motivation is the tendency to strive for success, persist in the fear of failure, and experience pride in accomplishments. Therefore in an athletic sports performance context, it is an athlete, overcoming barriers and obstacles, performing better than others and taking pride in taking part; for example, Wayne Price of Wakefield Wildcats rugby league team overcoming a double leg fracture to play again. Others may have felt that he did not have the drive to continue playing at an elite level again.

You are to conduct an interview with an athlete who you feel has overcome a barrier, for example returning to playing after injury, persistent in the face of failure (an athlete who still competes although they lose), or competes in an activity by seeking out opponents of better ability.

Within your interview you are to devise questions that will:

- Describe their motivations for participation
- Explain how motivations affect sports performance, positively or negatively
- Identify efforts involved in overcoming their barriers.

During your interview you will carry out the following survey:

Achievement motivation survey

Put a circle around the number that best matches your opinion about your participation in sporting activity.

Success in sport is very important to me	5 4 3 2 1	Winning doesn't matter; it's the game that counts
I prefer to play opponents that I know I can beat	1 2 3 4 5	I like playing opponents that are about my level
I enjoy a challenge	5 4 3 2 1	I like doing things I know I will succeed in
I don't enjoy close games	5 4 3 2 1	I enjoy a close game
I don't worry about the result of a game	1 2 3 4 5	I don't like telling people that I lost a game
I tend to make errors when I am under pressure	5 4 3 2 1	I play best when I am under pressure

Scoring

3–6 low achiever/avoider

7–10 average achiever/avoider

11–15 high achiever/avoider

Summarise the findings from your interview.

ACTIVITY 15

ATTRIBUTION THEORY

Three major factors affect how people explain the outcome of their behaviours, and their expectations for future behaviours, identify the psychological result of each factor of attribution.

Attribution theory	Psychological result
Stability:	Stability:
Stable (talent or good ability)	Stable
Unstable (good luck)	Unstable

Locus of causality:	Locus of causality:
Locus of causality:	Locus of causality:
Internal (Your effort in the last 50m of a race)	Internal
External (Easy field of competitors, do you try hard)	External

Locus of control:	Locus of control:
Locus of control:	Locus of control:
In one's control (drop out due to terrible talent)	In one's control
Outside of one's control (the cost of a programme)	Outside of one's control

LEARNING OUTCOME 2

2) Understand the relationships between stress, anxiety, arousal and sports performance

In this section we will focus on grading criteria P3 and M2 from Unit 16 – Psychology for Sports Performance.

ACTIVITY 16
DEFINITION

An understanding of stress is an important variable when considering the effect it has upon sports performance.

Think of a recent competition that you very much wanted to win. Try to recall how you felt before this competition started. Write down your answer.

The feelings you had are the symptoms of stress.

Definitions include:

'Any influence which disturbs the natural equilibrium of the body' (Wingate, 1982)

'Process whereby an individual perceives a threat and responds with a series of psychological and physiological changes including increased arousal and the experience of anxiety' (Javis, 1999)

ACTIVITY 17

TYPES OF STRESS

Research the following types of stress, use the activity to describe the effects on performance, include examples of sports performers.

- Eustress
- Distress
- Hyperstress
- Hypostress.

ACTIVITY 18

CAUSES OF STRESS

Complete the chart below, describing each of the causes of stress.

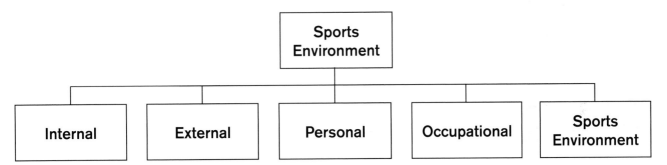

ACTIVITY 19

PERFORMANCE AND STRESS

Performance is related to stress levels. If stress levels are low, the sports performer will not feel motivated to perform to his or her optimum; this will therefore mean that the attention span of the sports performer is poor and short. As stress levels increase, so could the athlete's motivation and attention and therefore cause performance to improve. However, if the stress levels become too high, motivation and attention turn to panic, causing sports performance to drop off rapidly.

Working in pairs, ask your partner to design and deliver a coaching session to your class within ten minutes. Ensure your partner is wearing a heart rate monitor.

Ask how your partner feels right now, and write down their answer.

Observe and record his or her reactions to this stressful situation. Did your partner manage to complete the task? Explain the effects of stress on performance.

ACTIVITY 20

Anxiety   Competitive state anxiety inventory-2

	Not at all	Some what	Moder- ate	Very much so
1 I am concerned about this competition	1	2	3	4
2 I feel nervous	1	2	3	4
3 I feel at ease	1	2	3	4
4 I have self-doubts	1	2	3	4
5 I feel jittery	1	2	3	4
6 I feel comfortable	1	2	3	4
7 I am concerned that I may not do as well in this competition as I could	1	2	3	4
8 My body feels tense	1	2	3	4
9 I feel self-confident	1	2	3	4
10 I am concerned about losing	1	2	3	4
11 I feel tense in the stomach	1	2	3	4
12 I feel secure	1	2	3	4
13 I am concerned about choking under pressure	1	2	3	4
14 My body feels relaxed	1	2	3	4
15 I am confident I can meet the challenge	1	2	3	4
16 I am concerned about performing poorly	1	2	3	4
17 My heart is racing	1	2	3	4
18 I'm confident about performing well	1	2	3	4
19 I'm concerned about reaching my goal	1	2	3	4
20 I feel my stomach sinking	1	2	3	4
21 I feel mentally relaxed	1	2	3	4
22 I'm concerned that others will be disappointed with my performance	1	2	3	4
23 My hands are clammy	1	2	3	4
24 I'm confident because I mentally picture myself reaching my goal	1	2	3	4
25 I'm concerned I won't be able to concentrate	1	2	3	4
26 My body feels tight	1	2	3	4
27 I'm confident at coming through under pressure	1	2	3	4

Directions

A number of statements that athletes have used to describe their feelings before competitions are given above. Read each statement and then choose the appropriate number to the right of the statement to indicate **how you feel at present** – at this moment. There are no right or wrong answers. Do not spend too much time on any one statement, but choose the answer that describes **your feelings right now**.

Now complete the same questionnaire before an important sports performance, for example a cup final or a really important competition you want to win.

You should now have two copies of the questionnaire, one in a normal situation in the classroom and one for before an important sports performance. Use the scoring system below and record your data.

Scoring:

Cognitive Anxiety   1, 4, 7, 10, 13, 16, 19, 22, 25

Somatic Anxiety   2, 5, 8, 11, 14, 17, 20, 23, 26
(Reverse score N. 14)

Your scores – normal environment

Cognitive anxiety	
Somatic anxiety	

Your scores before sports performance

Cognitive anxiety	
Somatic anxiety	

Mean scores for the CSAI-2 by type of sport.

Sample	Mean score (cognitive anxiety)	Mean score (somatic anxiety)
Basketball	20.02	18.57
Cycling	20.51	18.89
Golf	16.97	15.31
Swimming	16.50	16.85
Track and field	20.34	18.73
Wrestling	17.74	19.90

Using the mean scores for the 'CSAI-2 by type of sport' table above, compare both your scores with those of the sports performers. In a table, try to explain the effects of anxiety on sports performance.

ACTIVITY 21

SYMPTOMS OF STRESS

This is a list of somatic physiological symptoms and cognitive psychological symptoms of stress.

Rearrange them into somatic physiological symptoms and cognitive psychological symptoms.

Worry or apprehension	Increased rate of speech
Increased heart rate	Increased blood pressure
Inability to concentrate	Irritability
Increased adrenaline	Increased blood sugar
Increased breathing rate	Aggression
Difficulty in making decisions	Increased perspiration

Somatic physiological symptoms	Cognitive psychological symptoms
1	1
2	2
3	3
4	4
5	5
6	6

England's football team has had an appalling record in penalty taking at both the World Cup and European Championship. Using two points from the somatic physiological symptoms and cognitive psychological symptoms above, explain the effects of those points on sports performance.

ACTIVITY 22

AROUSAL

Arousal is a term used for the intensity of the drive that is experienced by an athlete when trying to achieve a goal. High levels of arousal can result in both physiological and psychological symptoms. Arousal occurs across a continuum, from a deep sleep to very excited.

Label where you think the following terms would lie upon the arousal continuum. How would they make your feel?

1 Scoring the winning goal
2 Winning the lottery
3 Watching a history documentary
4 Hanging out with friends
5 Carrying out practical
6 Taking your first driving lesson.

Deep sleep → **Very excited**

ACTIVITY 23

THEORIES

By understanding the theories of arousal, a coach and athlete can recognise signs and symptoms of stress. This has important implications when preparing for sports performance.

Drive theory

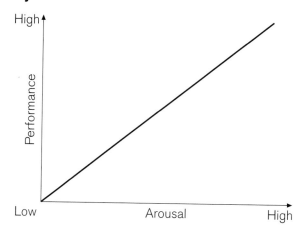

For an athlete of your choice, explain what happens to performance as arousal increases.

Inverted U hypothesis

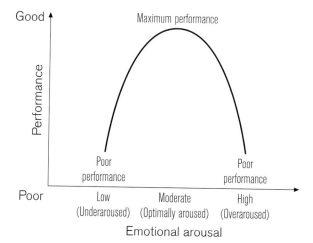

For an athlete of your choice, explain what happens to performance as arousal increases.

Catastrophe theory

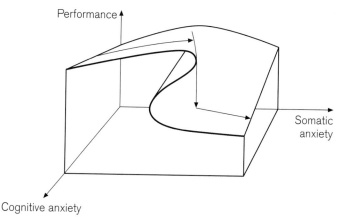

For an athlete of your choice, explain what happens to performance as arousal increases.

Zone of optimal functioning

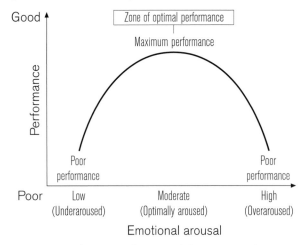

Explain the concept of 'zone of optimal functioning'.

ACTIVITY 24

You are working as an exercise psychologist consultant to an elite-level sports team. The manager has asked you to prepare a handout to give to the players that will advise them of changes that occur to the body while under the effects of stress. This handout will be useful as the players are currently in pre-season training. The manager recognises that a psychological understanding of stress for the players will improve their future performance.

Include in your handout:

Simple information about the sympathetic and parasympathetic nervous systems Say how the sympathetic nervous system produces a stress response on the player. Talk about how the sympathetic system can induce these effects upon a player:

- Increase in heart rate
- Increase in breathing rate
- Increase in metabolism
- Increase in heat production
- Increase in tension of the muscles
- Increase in adrenaline production.

Within your handout, try to explain how the above effects can affect your players' performance, explaining whether it is having a positive or negative effect on performance.

Increase in tension of the muscles

This could affect your player in this way: the player has too much muscle tension and when it comes to performing a simple pass of the ball, he/she would not be able to pass it to their team mate. Too much muscle tension could also cause injury – the player needs a certain degree of flexibility for movement. These would both cause a negative effect to performance. The player would need to control the levels of muscle tension to an appropriate level for successful performance.

How the parasympathetic nervous system produces a relaxation response to stress

The parasympathetic system can induce these effects upon a player:

- Slowed heart rate
- Slower breathing rate
- Muscle relaxation
- Lower body temperature
- Increase in saliva production
- Increase in dry skin.

Within your handout, try to explain how the above effects can affect your players' performance, again explaining whether each factor is having a positive or a negative effect on performance.

Slowed breathing rate

This could affect your player as follows: the player would be able to have a slow breathing rate when carrying out an important task, for example when taking a penalty. By being able to control their breathing rate, the player will be able to remain calm when shooting. This would have a positive effect on performance – the player would be able to place the ball where they wanted.

Changes to the sympathetic and parasympathetic nervous systems

Changes in attention focus

Maintaining attentional focus is vital for performance; by ensuring that a player can maintain their focus during a match, it will mean that they are not distracted by bad refereeing decisions, actions of both the crowd and the opposing team and by missed easy shots. By maintaining attention the players will become winners – a positive effect for performance.

Using the above as an example, try and explain what factors could affect your players' attention/focus. Explain whether they will be positive or negative effects on performance. And remember, your handout is for an elite sports team.

Choking

In the last season's cup final, the team missed a series of penalties, and in the final de-brief after the game the coach referred to 'choking'. On the bus back to their home ground, the coach overheard some of the players saying they did not understand this term. The coach wants to ensure that the players are clear about the term and can learn to recognise if it is about to occur. Research and include 'choking'.

MARKED ASSIGNMENTS

UNIT 3 – Training and Fitness for Sport

Training and Fitness for Sport (Unit 3)

SAMPLE ASSIGNMENT Number 1

Background unit information

Fitness is vital to achieving success in sport and any individual who is serious about their sports performance will use different methods to improve areas specific to the sport that they participate in.

Elite athletes develop and maintain high levels of fitness and take fitness training very seriously. It is therefore important to assess the fitness requirements in specific sports and ways in which sports performers can improve their own sports performance.

Fitness for sport

Scenario

Working for Sport Britain you have been asked to produce an information leaflet that will examine the different fitness requirements in three contrasting sports. The reasoning behind your task is to display to young children what areas of fitness they will need to work upon in order to become a successful sports performer.

With London 2012 in the horizon, Sport Britain has requested that you compile your leaflet on the following three Olympic sports:

- Track Athletics (middle distance)
- Football
- Tennis

Your assignment will provide assessment evidence for the following:

Learning outcomes	Learning outcomes 1 and 2
Identified grading criteria	P1, P2, M1, M2, D1

WHAT YOU NEED TO DO

In this assessment you will need to produce an information leaflet that describes the physical fitness requirements and skill-related fitness requirements of track athletics (middle distance), football and tennis.

Produce a report for your local authority that will describe methods of training appropriate for various components of physical fitness.

TASKS

Task 1

On your leaflet you should display images of elite sports performers from the sports listed below, and next to these images you should describe the **physical fitness requirements and skill-related fitness requirements** for each of the following sports:

- **Track Athletics (middle distance)**
- **Football**
- **Tennis**

(P1)

> **TIP:** To **describe** something you should try and paint a picture in words for the reader. It is useful to think that the reader of your script knows nothing and therefore you have to teach what you know using words on paper.
>
> Ensure you cover all the key features of the point that you are describing.

In order to achieve the merit criterion of this task, as well as completing the pass criterion of the above task you must also:

Explain the physical fitness requirements and skill-related fitness requirements of each of the following sports:

- **Track Athletics (middle distance)**
- **Football**
- **Tennis**

TIP: To **explain** you should discuss, using examples, how each component of fitness you have described should be fully utilised and how elite athletes from the world of sport actually use the specific component of fitness to maximise their own sports performance.

In order to achieve the distinction criterion in this task, as well as completing the above tasks you must also:

Compare and contrast the physical fitness requirements and skill-related fitness requirements of track athletics, football and tennis.

(D1)

TIP: When **comparing and contrasting** the fitness requirements of each sport you should attempt to describe what components of fitness are used in all three of the sports and discuss how each sport uses each requirement. Then, also explain the requirements that may be needed in some of the sports but not in others, and explain why you think this to be the case.

Scenario

Your leaflet has been a success and now Sport Britain has been inundated with young children who are looking to enhance their own physical fitness to help them improve their sports performance.

Due to the level of demand local sports centres have asked you to provide them with examples of the methods of training that you would advise them to use in order to improve specific components of fitness.

Your brief from the local authority is to provide local leisure centres with one method of training for each of the following components of fitness:

- Flexibility
- Strength
- Muscular endurance
- Power
- Aerobic endurance
- Speed

Produce your findings in a report for the local leisure centres to use as professional development training for their employees.

Task 2

Describe one method of fitness training for the following components of physical fitness:

- Flexibility
- Strength
- Muscular endurance
- Power
- Aerobic endurance
- Speed

(P2)

TIP: To **describe** something you should try and paint a picture in words for the reader. It is useful to think that the reader of your script knows nothing and therefore you have to teach the reader what you know using words on paper.

Ensure you cover all the key features of the point that you are describing.

In order to achieve the merit criterion of this task, as well as completing the pass criterion of the above task you must also:

Explain one method of fitness training for the following components of physical fitness

- Flexibility
- Strength
- Muscular endurance
- Power
- Aerobic endurance
- Speed

(M2)

TIP: To **explain** you should discuss, using examples, how each method of training could enhance each of the different components of physical fitness. You should try and use appropriate examples of how these methods have enhanced sports performance of elite athletes or your own personal experiences.

GRADING GUIDANCE

For all the identified grading criteria you will need to:

Pass criteria

P1 describe the physical fitness requirements and skill-related fitness requirements of three different sporting activities

P2 describe one method of fitness training for six different components of physical fitness

Merit criteria

M1 explain the physical fitness requirements and skill-related fitness requirements of three different sporting activities

M2 explain one method of fitness training for six different components of physical fitness

Distinction criterion

D1 compare and contrast the physical fitness requirements and skill-related fitness requirements of three different sporting activities

When you have completed Tasks 1 and 2 you should consider the following:

How do you think you have done in the assignment?

Using the assessment criteria grid that you have already been issued with, please **highlight in pencil where you feel you have met each criterion within the assignment.** For example, highlight where you think you have met the criteria for P1.

129

ASSESSOR FEEDBACK FORM

Course: BTEC National Sport   Unit: Training and Fitness for Sport

Assignment number: One   Tutor:

Student name: Date:

Grading criteria achieved
Please tick the grading criteria assessed and achieved in this assignment.
Put a cross if the grading criteria has not been achieved.

Pass	Assessed	Achieved	Merit	Assessed	Achieved	Distinction	Assessed	Achieved
P1			M1			D1		
P2			M2			D2		
P3			M3					
P4								
P5								

Tutor feedback

Action plan for future assignments (To be completed by the learner)

Signed: (Tutor)   Date:

Signed: (Learner)   Date:

Signed: (Internal Verifier)   Date:

BTEC National in Sport

Student name: ....

Unit Number and Title	Training and Fitness for Sport
Assignment Number and Title	1 Fitness for Sport
Unit Tutor	Mark Adams
Assignment Issue Date	October 1st
Assignment Submission Date	October 28th
Internal Verifier	
Date Internally Verified	
Assignment Fit for Purpose (IV Signature)	

PASS LEVEL ANSWER

Task 1

Physical fitness requirements and Skill-related fitness

London 2012
Olympic
Track Athletes
Football
Tennis

Physical fitness requirements and
Skill-related fitness requirements

sport BRITAIN

www.sportbritain.org.uk

This leaflet has been produced by Sport Britain for children to see what different fitness requirements are required for Track Athletics (middle distance running), Football and Tennis.

PASS LEVEL ANSWER

Task 1

Physical Fitness and Skill Related Fitness Requirements

Kelly Holmes
Physical Fitness Requirements

Aerobic Endurance: is needed for a middle distance runner to maintain performance.

Muscular Endurance: Is needed to ensure the runner can maintain muscular contractions especially in the legs.

Flexibility: Is needed to maintain stride pattern around the hip, it also needed for shoulder and arm drive.

Speed: is needed to be able to produce fast movement at the start of the race and the sprint finish.

Strength: a minimal amount of strength is required, strength is needed for holding position during the race.

Power: is needed in the legs for drive.

Body Composition: will need to be ectomorphs, and not carry extra weight which will slow them down when running

Skill Related Fitness Requirements

Agility: Will be needed to change direction during running

Balance: is required to keep an upright body position

Co-ordination: is needed as there are other athletes in the race, the runner must ensure they do not make contact with them.

Reaction time: Needed at the start, for when responding to the gun.

David Beckham Football Player
Physical Fitness Requirements

Aerobic Endurance: is important as the game lasts 90 mins, a player needs to keep going.

Muscular Endurance: is needed to maintain leg movements.

Flexibility: is needed for movements around the hips when tackling

Speed: is required to get to a player or a pass

Strength: is necessary to fend of the opposition when shielding the ball

Power: is for jumping to the ball.

Body Composition: a footballer will be required to carry no extra weight as this will slow them down when playing

Skill Related Fitness Requirements

Agility: is required to change direction quickly for a pass or a tackle

Balance: a footballer will often be on one leg when passing or shooting, they must maintain it to reduce errors

Co-ordination: is essential for performance, coordinating leg movements and the ball is vital in dribbling the ball.

Reaction Time: is important to respond to your opponents and team mates quickly.

Andrew Murray
Physical Fitness Requirements

Aerobic Endurance: is essential, games are often played for long periods and also in warm weather.

Muscular Endurance: is necessary for hitting the ball.

Flexibility: is required when stretching for a return shot.

Speed: is vital for movement around the court.

Strength: the ability to maintain force many times, i.e. hitting the ball.

Power: is required for putting through to a shot

Body Composition: low levels of body at are needed, extra weight will slow the tennis player down around the court.

Skill Related Fitness Requirements

Agility: is needed for responding to your opponents shot selection

Balance: Being off balance will mean you shot will not be placed correctly.

Co-ordination: is vital, you need to coordinate the tennis ball with your arm movements for a correct shot

Reaction Time: is required for being ready for a shot.

133

Task 2

LOCAL AUTHORITY LEISURE CENTRE
PROFESSIONAL DEVELOPMENT TRAINING

METHODS OF TRAINING TO IMPROVE
COMPONENTS OF FITNESS

Assignment 1 Task 2 – Describe one method of fitness training for the following components of fitness (P2)

FLEXIBILITY – Stretching is the main method of improving flexibility, to do this effectively you can use static stretching methods:

• Static stretching – hold the stretch for 10 to 15 secs with no movement

STRENGTH – To develop strength you can use weight resistance machines doing a specified number of sets and repetitions for different parts of the body

MUSCULAR ENDURANCE – To develop muscular endurance you could use resistance machines for all the different body parts as in developing strength but do higher amounts of repetitions with lower weights

POWER – To improve power in the legs you could use standing jump exercises and bounding exercises over small hurdles or other objects of a similar height

AEROBIC ENDURANCE – To improve aerobic endurance you could use continuous training which includes exercising non-stop for longer periods of time. Eg 15 minute run on the treadmill, stepper or bike.

SPEED – Speed can be developed through Roll and Run drills. Place a cone at 15 metres and another at 30 metres. Steadily jog to cone 1 then sprint to cone two walking back. This would be repeated a number of times.

ASSESSOR FEEDBACK FORM

BTEC NATIONAL DIPLOMA IN SPORTS STUDIES

ASSESSMENT REPORT	**Unit:** Training and Fitness (Unit 3) Assignment 1 Fitness for Sport	**Lecturer:**

STUDENT NAME:	Learner 1

GENERAL COMMENTS

Well done. You have displayed general levels of understanding in this assignment. You have successfully described one method of fitness training for the components of fitness, gaining criterion P2. Although you could have expanded on your answers you show certain levels of awareness on fitness training for the components of fitness.

Your poster was generally well presented and informative. You successfully studied three elite sports performers and described their physical fitness requirements in their individual sporting activities. Again, you correctly identified the major components of fitness and described them and then correctly related them to the performer. Therefore you have successfully achieved P1 of the assessed grading criteria.

All of the available pass criteria have been awarded. Please see the action box below for details on how to upgrade this assignment.

ASSESSMENT CRITERIA	ACHIEVED
P1 Describe the physical fitness requirements and skill-related fitness requirements of three different sporting activities	**YES**/NO
P2 Describe one method of fitness training for six different components of physical fitness	**YES**/NO
M1 Explain the physical fitness requirements and skill-related fitness requirements of three different sporting activities	YES/**NO**
M2 Explain one method of fitness training for six different components of physical fitness	YES/**NO**
D1 Compare and contrast the physical fitness requirements and skill-related fitness requirements of three different sporting activities	YES/**NO**

ACTION

In order to achieve all of the available grading criteria you must:

M1 – explain (provide details and give reasons to support your opinion) the physical fitness requirements and skill-related fitness requirements of three different sporting activities

M2 – explain (provide details and give reasons to support your opinion) one method of fitness training for six different components of physical fitness

D1 – compare and contrast (identify the main factors that apply and explain the similarities and differences or the advantages and disadvantages) the physical requirements and skill-related fitness requirements for three different sporting activities

None of the above was included in your work and therefore you could not possibly be awarded M1, M2 and D1 of the assessed grading criteria.

MERIT LEVEL ANSWER

Training and Fitness for Sport (Unit Number 3)
ASSIGNMENT 1 Fitness for Sport

P1 describe the physical fitness requirements and skill-related fitness requirements of three different sporting activities

+

M1 explain the physical fitness requirements and skill-related fitness requirements of three different sporting activities

FOR THIS PART OF THE ASSIGNMENT I WILL EXPLAIN THE PHYSICAL FITNESS REQUIREMENTS AND SKILL RELATED FITNESS REQUIREMENTS FOR DIFFERENT SPORTS. THE SPORTS THAT I WILL EXPLAIN ARE:

- Track Athletics (middle distance)
- Football
- Tennis

Fitness can be defined as "The ability to carry out our daily tasks without undue fatigue". (Davis, Bull, Roscoe & Roscoe (1994). A sports person is required to train and compete on a regular basis, due to this their 'daily tasks' require higher fitness levels than sedentary people. If they are to meet the demands of their sport a player must train and focus on meeting all the components of fitness that relate to their sport. There are many components of fitness and these can be broken down into 2 main types, these are:

- Physical fitness
- Skill-related fitness

Physical Fitness Components

- **Aerobic endurance:** aerobic endurance is also called stamina. It is the ability of the body to maintain exercise over a period of time. It relates to how well the body can supply oxygen to the muscles for fuel.
- **Muscular endurance:** this component of fitness can be broken down to local and general muscular endurance.
- **Flexibility:** this relates to the range of movement possible at a joint. Flexibility is important in a number of sports as it enables the body to move in various ways.
- **Speed:** is the ability of the body to cover a short distance in the lowest time.
- **Strength:** is the ability of the body to exert maximum force.
- **Body composition:** this is the shape of the body and is made up of three components: mesomorph (muscular) ectomorph, (thin) endomorph (fat).

Skill-related fitness components include:

- **Agility:** this is a combination of speed and change of direction.
- **Balance:** the ability to keep control of your body position. This can be either dynamic (involving movement – walking / jumping on a balance beam) or static (keeping still – standing on 1 leg).
- **Co-ordination:** the ability to move the body efficiently and affectively in the desired manner.
- **Power:** the ability of the body to exert a maximal muscular contraction in an explosive burst (e.g. a jump).
- **Reaction time:** this is how quickly the brain can respond to a stimulus and move the muscular system as a response.

There is not an ideal overall fitness level to suit everyone. Having the correct components of fitness to suit your sport is the most important thing. It is vital that an athlete trains the areas of the body and the specific fitness components that are specific to their sport. For example, a rugby player needs to change direction to try and avoid being tackled so agility is very important. On the other hand a marathon runner wouldn't need to change direction fast, so agility should not be a key requirement in their training regime. Training for the exact components that are needed for your sport is called **specificity**.

Track Athletics (middle distance)

- **Aerobic endurance:** this is a vital component for a middle distance athlete because any activity lasting more than a couple of minutes will be predominantly aerobic. Events include 800m, 1500m and 3000m for runners and wheelchair athletes and steeplechase for runners.
- **Muscular endurance:** the main muscles involved in middle distance are the legs. Due to the repeated contraction of these muscles muscular endurance is important, however the main component will be aerobic endurance.
- **Flexibility:** For a middle distance runner flexibility is most important for the movement of the hips and shoulders, as these joints propel the athlete through the running motion. General flexibility of all the main synovial joints will mean the athlete can move efficiently through the running motion.
- **Speed:** this component is very important. To win races athletes are often required to produce a sprint finish, reaching high speeds. As well as aerobic endurance good middle distance runners will also be fast.
- **Strength:** this is not as important for a middle distance runner as they are not required to move large weights, they may sometimes need some strength to hold their position if they are in a bunch of athletes.

- **Power:** this is not an essential component to the success in middle distance, some middle distance athletes will have good power levels, mainly in their legs, probably due to general muscular fitness.
- **Body composition:** middle distance runners will mainly be ectomorphs and mesomorphs as they do not want to carry excessive weight around the track. They will have relatively defined muscles of the legs, arms and trunk due to their repeated movements of those parts of the body in competition and training.

Skill-related fitness components include:

- **Agility:** sometimes an athlete may need to change direction quickly for example if an athlete falls in a race and you need to avoid them requiring agility.
- **Balance:** endurance athlete will not require excellent balance like a gymnast, however, some balance to remain on their optimum running line and to keep their body posture straight is a bonus.
- **Co-ordination:** coordination of the muscle contraction to enable the correct movements in the correct order will be needed. The movements do not require the high coordination levels such as games players e.g. ball skills etc.
- **Reaction time:** reacting to the gun at the beginning of a race and also reacting to the other athletes if they make a move to the front or sprint off are the times that reaction time is important to middle distance athletes.

Football

- **Aerobic endurance:** a game of football lasts 90 minutes or longer if extra time and penalties are needed. For this reason a large amount of aerobic endurance is needed to be able to last the whole game.
- **Muscular endurance:** the repeated actions of jumping, tackling passing and running will demand high levels of muscular endurance, particularly in the legs.
- **Flexibility:** this will be needed particularly for lunging in tackles in the lower body and throwing in the upper body. General range of movement will be needed for all activities during the game.
- **Speed:** this is important for player to get past the opposition and also get to opposition players to make a tackle. Much of the game of football will involve short sprints. Some players will require more speed than others (eg a striker compared to a goal keeper).
- **Strength:** this will be required when shielding the ball from other players and shoulder charging.
- **Power:** power in the legs will be important for jumping to head the ball. Also shooting and kicking the ball a long way will need power.

- **Body composition:** this can be very different for most players. Generally a football player will be a mesomorph, however, a balance between ectomorph and endomorph is needed so that the player is not too fat or skinny.
- **Agility:** this is a vital component to all football players as they need to change direction in both defence and attack, to react to opposition players or to try and beat them.
- **Balance:** if a player is off balance during passing, shooting or tackling they will not produce the desired outcome. For this reason
- **Co-ordination:** timing of the movement of all your body parts is critical to footballing success. Demonstrating the range of footballing skills (eg passing, tackling etc) will involve highly coordinated muscular motion.
- **Reaction time:** this is very important for all football players as you are continually having to react to other players on the pitch from your own team and the opposition. A goal keeper would need a particularly good reaction time to save shots (eg a penalty kick).

Tennis

- **Aerobic endurance:** some tennis matches can last several hours and the majority of the time is spent playing. For this reason high levels of aerobic endurance are critical for success.
- **Muscular endurance:** this is very important during a rally as players are required to repeat shots involving muscular endurance in the shoulder.
- **Flexibility:** this is very important in both the upper and lower body. A player will need to lunge for various shots (needing high levels of hip movements). Also shoulder movements are important to be able to apply a range of different shots.
- **Speed:** a rally in tennis may require many sprints depending on the duration. Depending on the style of the player (eg serve volley or baseline) may change the length of time in a rally requiring different levels of speed endurance.
- **Strength:** this is important in tennis to be able to keep the correct body posture during the game. It is not as important as football however.
- **Body composition:** tennis players will be mesomorphs to allow them to be muscular enough to play the powerful shots involved in competition and training. They will be low in endomorphy, so they do not need to carry excess weight and different levels of ectomorphy due to different styles of play and anatomical differences.

Skill-related fitness components include:

- **Power:** this is a fundamental aspect of a tennis player's game, particularly at top level, as a powerful shot can beat an opponent in a rally. A well placed powerful serve can often result in an ace. All tennis shots will require power

- **Agility:** this is extremely important to a tennis player as you need to change direction many times in a rally and cover all areas of the court quickly.
- **Balance:** a player needs to be balanced when playing a shot as all the body parts need to be in the correct position or you will be off balance and this will negatively affect the shot. This is particularly important in serving, due to the complexity of the skill.
- **Co-ordination:** striking a tennis ball using the correct technique and shot selection requires a high level of hand-eye coordination. This is increased further in the sport of tennis as coordinating the racket with the motion of the arm requires a high ability and skill level.
- **Reaction time:** reacting to an opponents shot is crucial to success in tennis. The time it takes a player to respond and the move to a players shot will result in either success or failure.

P2 describe one method of fitness training for six different components of physical fitness

+

M2 explain one method of fitness training for six different components of physical fitness

The following section of this assignment will explain how up and coming athletes, with their sights on the Olympics in 2012, should train to meet the demands of their sport. As already mentioned specificity is a term that relates to the specific demands of your sport. Different areas of fitness must be focused on in training to increase the areas of fitness that relate to an athletes chosen sport. There are many different types of training and this section of my assignment will explain a training method to develop the following fitness components:

- FLEXIBILITY
- STRENGTH
- MUSCULAR ENDURANCE
- POWER
- AEROBIC ENDURANCE
- SPEED

FLEXIBILITY

FLEXIBILITY IS A VITAL ASPECT OF FITNESS FOR MANY SPORT AND EXERCISE ACTIVITIES. TO DEVELOP FLEXIBILITY STRETCHING YOUR MUSCLES WILL INCREASE THE RANGE OF MOVEMENT AT YOUR JOINTS. THERE ARE 3 MAIN TYPES OF STRETCHING, THESE ARE:

- Static stretching (involving no movement)
- Ballistic stretching (involving movement)
- PROPRIOCEPTIVE NEUROMUSCULAR FACILITATION (PNF) STRETCHING

Stretching is an important ingredient of any warm-up and cool-down and will minimise the risk of injury. Also, some training activities can help with flexibility apart from just warming up and cooling down.

Quadriceps Stretch

Using a static stretching method (e.g. the quadriceps stretch shown above) a person should:

- Hold your foot with your hand whilst pulling your foot upwards
- Keep your posture straight
- Extend your toe
- Hold the stretch for 10–15 seconds (more in a cool down)
- Make sure you repeat this for the other side of the body

STRENGTH

To develop strength many athletes will use a variety of resistance machines. Some examples that you will find in a gym include:

- Shoulder Press
- Chest Press
- Lat Pull downs
- Lower Back Extensions
- Triceps Press
- Calf Raise
- Biceps Curls
- Leg Curls

- Leg Extension
- Leg Press
- Sit Ups

Taken from http://www.brianmac.demon.co.uk/conwtgn.htm

To develop your strength for competition and muscle size you include repetitions of the same exercise (e.g. 10 bicep curls) and repeat this after a short rest period. Each group of 10 reps is called a set.

To increase your strength you need to apply training principles by progressively increasing either the weights lifted or the number of sets and reps you include and decrease rest periods.

Muscular endurance

Muscular endurance combines both aerobic and anaerobic components. To develop muscular endurance you should include repeated exercises using the same muscle group/s (e.g. sit ups, press ups and resistance machines). If you use resistance machines to develop muscular endurance you should use less resistance (weight) than you would use for developing strength (e.g. more than 12 repetitions). As with strength training the concept of sets and reps can be applied.

Power

Platform depth jumps are a method of developing muscular power in the legs. Participants should stand on a small box and step off landing on both feet and then jump onto the higher box as quickly as possible. See the diagram below. As your power improves you can increase the height of the box as a method of progression.

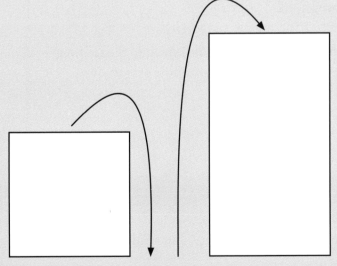

Aerobic endurance

Any activity lasting more that a couple of minutes of continuous exercise will be mainly aerobic. Middle and long distance runners, cyclists and swimmers are examples. To develop aerobic endurance you need to increase the duration of training sessions compared to other activities. To train you can perform continuous or interval training. Continuous training involves training non-stop for long periods of time (e.g. running or swimming) at low or moderate intensity. Many athletes may use a heart rate monitor to make sure they remain in their optimum heart rate zone (eg 60-70%).

Speed

This is a vital component for many sports and there are various ways to develop speed. Resistance sprints are a method often used by top athletes during training. A harness is attached around the waist of a sprinter with a resistance attached to straps attached to it. These can be weights that you pull along the ground or a parachute (see diagram below). If repeated sprints are used with resistance during training this can develop speed in competition.

All the methods of training that have been described must include the training principles to achieve success. These are specificity, reversibility, progressive overload.

Bibliography

http://www.brianmac.demon.co.uk/conwtgn.htm

Davis B., Bull R., Roscoe J. & Roscoe D. (2000) *Physical Education and the Study of Sport*. Mosby.

www.manitobainmotion.ca/.../10_standing.gif

www.biggerfasterstronger.com/uploads/C-Giant-Sprint-Chute-Side-V.jpg

ASSESSOR FEEDBACK FORM

BTEC NATIONAL DIPLOMA IN SPORTS STUDIES

ASSESSMENT REPORT	**Unit:** Training and Fitness (Unit 3) Assignment 1 Fitness for Sport	**Lecturer:**

STUDENT NAME:	Learner 2

GENERAL COMMENTS

You have made a good attempt at this assignment. Your work illustrates sound levels of both knowledge and understanding. You successfully described (P1) and explained (M1) the physical fitness and skill-related fitness requirements for three different sporting activities. Athletics, football and tennis are all covered individually and in detail. Each sport is broken down into physical and skill related fitness components in an orderly way. Your understanding of fitness training for six differing components of fitness is also evident in your work. You have again described (P2) and explained (M2) one method of fitness training for six different components of physical fitness well with good use of diagrams in your work.

This is a good assignment. Please see action points below on how to improve your work; nevertheless this was a good piece of work.

ASSESSMENT CRITERIA	ACHIEVED
P1 Describe the physical fitness requirements and skill-related fitness requirements of three different sporting activities	**YES**/NO
P2 Describe one method of fitness training for six different components of physical fitness	**YES**/NO
M1 Explain the physical fitness requirements and skill-related fitness requirements of three different sporting activities	**YES**/NO
M2 Explain one method of fitness training for six different components of physical fitness	**YES**/NO
D1 Compare and contrast the physical fitness requirements and skill-related fitness requirements of three different sporting activities	YES/**NO**

ACTION

You have failed to achieve D1.

D1 – In order to achieve this you must compare and contrast (identify the main factors that apply and explain the similarities and differences or the advantages and disadvantages) both the physical requirements, and skill-related fitness requirements of three different sporting activities.

DISTINCTION LEVEL ANSWER

Task 1

FITNESS REQUIREMENTS IN SPORT

*A LOOK AT
ATHLETICS
FOOTBALL
TENNIS*

Sport Britain

Tel: 555 555 5555

---

sport BRITAIN

FITNESS REQUIREMENTS IN SPORT

Primary Business Address
Sport Britain
Fitness Road
Smalltown

Phone: 555-555-5555
Fax: 555-555-5555

Email: xyz@microsoft.com

Roger Federer Fitness Requirements

Muscular Endurance: Required for playing shots for up to 3 hour matches

Aerobic Endurance: Required for effective performance in matches lasting long periods

Flexibility: required in upper and lower body to reach and lunge for different shots

Speed: Required as it is a high speed game played in a relatively small area. Needed to get to and make shots.

Strength: required in core to maintain good posture for technique and upper body for effective shots.

Power: Needed for shots to win the rally and point eg serve and volley

Body Composition: Need to be muscular to enable powerful shots and lean to be mobile around the court.

Skill Related Fitness Requirements

Agility: Needed to respond to opponents shots

Balance: Needs good balance to technically hit the ball correctly

Co-ordination: Hand eye co-ordination to hit a variety of tennis shots.

Reaction time: Needed to react to opponents shot selection

DISTINCTION LEVEL ANSWER

Task 1

PHYSICAL AND SKILL RELATED FITNESS REQUIREMENTS

Physical Fitness Requirements of Mo Farah [athletics]

Muscular Endurance: needed to keep the muscles working effectively from start to finish maintaining technique.

Aerobic endurance: Needed to complete the distance in a certain time maintaining performance

Flexibility: Helps deliver an effective stride pattern through the hips and legs and when driving the arms and shoulders

Strength: Needed in core stability to maintain technique and upper body to hold your race position

Body Composition: Needs to be slim and toned (ectomorphs) with no excess weight for maximum efficiency.

Speed: Needed for maximum arm and le drive for sprint finish

Power: Needed in the legs for sprint finishes

Skill Related Fitness for Mo Farah

Agility: Needed to change direction when overtaking competitors

Balance: needed to maintain running lines and posture

Co-ordination: needed to deliver an effective and efficient running style

Reaction time: Reacting to the gun or to other athletes movements in the race.

Physical fitness requirements of Steven Gerrard [footballer]

Muscular Endurance: Needed to keep the muscles working effectively from start of match to finish.

Aerobic Endurance: Needed to last the full 90 minutes maintaining performance

Flexibility: Needed for stretching when tackling

Strength:Needed to hold off opponents when keep possession of the ball.

Body composition: Need to be well toned with no extra weight to maintain performance for full 90 mins

Speed:Needed for a striker to get passes a defender

Power: Required in the legs to strike a ball when shooting

Skill Related Fitness for Steven Gerrard

Agility: required to change direction quickly to receive a pass or to make a tackle

Balance: required to dribble the ball at speed

Co-ordination: Required for striking the ball to make an effective pass or shot

Reaction Time: Required to react to opponents actions eg intercepting a pass, saving a shot or timing a tackle

FITNESS REQUIREMENTS IN SPORT

Primary Business Address
Sport Britain
Fitness Road
Smalltown

Phone: 555-555-5555
Fax: 555-555-5555
Email: xyz@microsoft.com

147

Training and Fitness for Sport
Unit Number 3
Assignment Number 1
Fitness for Sport Task 1

P1 describe the physical fitness requirements and skill related fitness requirements of three different sporting activities

See included leaflet.

M1 explain the physical fitness requirements and skill related fitness requirements of three different sporting activities

Physical Fitness Requirements for a Track Athlete (middle distance)

Aerobic Endurance: this is a vital element for the middle distance track athlete. A middle distance athlete requires aerobic endurance due to the nature of the events that come under the title of "middle distance" these continuous running events may include, 800 metres, 1500 metres, 3000 metres and 3000 metre steeplechase. These events can last up to 30 mins depending on the event and the ability of the athlete, and therefore involve oxygen intake at all time.

Muscular Endurance: is essential in middle distance running, the athlete will need to maintain muscular endurance throughout the race. Muscular contractions will occur throughout the race as the athlete continues to move from the start to finish.

Flexibility: a good level of flexibility is needed due to the movements involved in running. Flexibility around the hip is required as a stride pattern is essential in running. It will also be needed for shoulder drive and arm movement. This especially evident when the athlete starts a race, i.e. the athlete will need to produce power for movement, produced through the movement of the shoulders and arms.

Speed: is required when there is a need for a fast movement, in the start it is essential that the athlete gets away from the line, so that they have good track position. Sprinting may also be required if there is a "sprint finish" for the line, where the athlete has to increase speed for a final push to the line to beat any opposing athletes challenging for the finish.

Strength: a minimal amount of strength is required for middle distance running, it can be argued that an athlete may need some strength when holding for position or when making their way through the field.

Power: a minimal amount of power is also required for performance. Levels of power are needed in the legs of the athlete, for basic running movement and in the case of the steeplechase; power is required for hurdling the barriers and coming out of the water jump.

Body Composition: the amount of bodyweight an athlete carriers will affect their performance, if an athlete has excess bodyweight it will make it harder for them to perform efficiently. Athletes will tend to have ectomorphoic body composition with some degree of mesomorphic due to them having muscles required for movements.

Skill Related Fitness Requirements for a Track Athlete (middle distance)

Agility: is needed for performance, because an athlete will need to change direction when running, for example when at the start, an athlete will have to ensure they do not make contact with other athletes. This is due to the athlete not being assigned a lane position as in sprinting, it is a massed start. During a race the athlete will need agility to respond to other athletes movements.

Balance: is required to maintain the body in an upright position, by keeping the correct body position while running, the athlete will be more streamlined and will therefore not lose energy.

Co-ordination: is needed by the athlete, this will ensure that they do not make contact with other athletes; any contact is likely to slow the athlete down and interrupt the running style.

Reaction Time: is essential in athletic performance, reacting to the gun is vital; the athlete needs to get good track position for the race. An athlete may also have to respond to any other athletes in the race, i.e. when they make a move to the front of the pack or strike for home in a sprint finish.

Physical Fitness Requirements for a football player

Aerobic Endurance: is vital for a football player, the game can last 90 mins, it is essential that the player has the aerobic endurance to keep going all the way to the end of the match. Games have often been won in added time, when opposing players have tired, and the aerobically endurance fitter teams have scored.

Muscular Endurance: is crucial in football, football has plenty of repeated movements involving the legs of the player, for example, running, passing, tackling and shooting. It is clear that a player must have muscular endurance to keep on performing time after time.

Flexibility: is essential for football, players need good range of motion around the hips (for running and tackling movements) and around the shoulders also (when throwing the ball) A goal keeper may need higher levels of flexibility compared to a normal player. The goalkeeper may be required to tip the ball around or over the bar.

Speed: is critical for positive performance, a player will need to have speed of movement to get to a pass, when dribbling with the ball or to track back and make a tackle of an opponent.

Strength: is important for the football player, the player will need to ensure they can shield the ball, for example when trying to prevent the opposing player getting to the ball and saving the resulting corner or throw in.

Power: is needed for when the player is required to jump off the ground to make a header or make a shot. The amount of power production will depend on the goal of the skill, clearing the ball a long way or small distance pass.

Body Composition: a football player will not want to carry out any extra weight; any excess will result in the player having to work harder than someone who does not carry any extra bodyweight. The football will have a mesomorph body composition.

Skill Related Fitness Requirements for a football player

Agility: is an essential factor for successful football performance. A footballer will be required to change direction many times during the game, for both a pass and a tackle.

Balance: a footballer will often be on one leg when passing or shooting the ball. The player must maintain balance to reduce errors. For example when a player is off balance and they go for a shot a goal, the ball will not travel in the direction the player wished the ball to travel in.

Co-ordination: is vital, being able to coordinate leg movements when in possession of the ball is needed when dribbling with the ball.

Reaction Time: as football is a two team sport, the player will need to respond to several stimulus throughout the game, for example, the ball, an opposing player or a team mate, the quicker the player can respond the quicker they will get into the correct position.

Physical Fitness Requirements for a Tennis Player

Aerobic Endurance: is essential for a tennis player, tennis games are often played over long periods of time and in hot weather also. The tennis player who can perform longer than their opponent is more likely to succeed.

Muscular Endurance: is necessary as players will be required to work the same muscles groups when playing a rally. The muscles of the arms, shoulders and back will be used numerous times when hitting the ball.

Flexibility: the tennis player who has good levels of flexibility will be able to stretch for a shot and move to the next shot efficiently.

Speed: is vital for good court position, the player may have to respond to a variety of shots, including a drop or a lob, possessing the speed will enable the player to get into position.

Strength: the ability to apply a force and maintain the force throughout the game is crucial. For example applying strength to a similar shot through the game, the same levels should occur through the whole game.

Power: is needed when selecting the amount of power into the shot. Certain types of shot will require greater levels of power than others. Tennis players, who play a base line game, will require repeated powerful shots to propel the ball to the far end of the court. Others, who play a service game, will require a powerful serve, so that an opposing player can not return the serve.

Body Composition: the player will not carry excess body weight; extra will slow movement around the court. The tennis player is likely to have a body composition that is mesomorph and have ectomorph tendencies, as having extra length in appendices will increase force and power production in shot making. Extra length in the levers will allow the players not to move as much around the court compared to a smaller player.

Skill Related Fitness Requirements for a Tennis Player

Agility: is needed for the player to respond to a variety of shot selections from your opponent.

Balance: being of balance for the tennis player will ensure that the desired location of the shot will not occur. Having a stable centre of gravity will aid in shot production and desired placement of the ball in your opposing court.

Co-ordination: is vital, you need to be able to coordinate the arm movements of the player with the tennis balls movements. If coordination is wrong, a shot can be miss hit, the resulting action is that the ball can end up not in the correct desired location.

Reaction Time: is crucial, the tennis player who has the quicker reaction time will be able to respond quicker, therefore they can respond to and get into the correct position, and they will have extra time to process the demands of the activity.

D1 Compare and contrast the physical fitness requirement and skill related fitness requirements of three different sporting activities

This table indicates where physical and skill related fitness occur in athletics, football and tennis.

	Athletics	Football	Tennis
Physical Fitness Requirements			
Aerobic Endurance	✓	✓	✓
Muscular Endurance	✓	✓	✓
Flexibility	✓	✓	✓
Speed	✓	✓	✓
Strength	✓	✓	✓
Power	✓	✓	✓
Body Composition	✓	✓	✓
Skill Related Fitness Requirements			
Agility	✓	✓	✓
Balance	✓	✓	✓
Co-ordination	✓	✓	✓
Reaction Time	✓	✓	✓

As you can see from the above table, all the physical and skill related factors occur in athletics, football and tennis. The important factor for each sport is how much each of the physical and skill related factors contribute for successful performance in each of the sports.

This section will compare and contrast each of these physical and skill related factors for the three sports, athletics, football and tennis.

Aerobic Endurance: This is an important factor for all the sports, oxygen intake and capacity to perform is vital for all the sports. In athletics, the need will depend on the middle distance event; each distance will have different demands of aerobic endurance, middle distance running can last up to 30 mins. In football aerobic endurance is also important the ability to maintain performance throughout the game is vital, football game is 90 mins in length. In tennis, aerobic endurance is also very important, A tennis game can go for long periods of times, up to 4 hours is common place, although in tennis, the player has rest periods between games and sets, in football the player will be performing for the full game, however there will be periods of play where the player is working a low percentage of their aerobic capacity, and in comparison in athletics the athlete will have no periods of rest, or low intensity work as in football and tennis and they will perform for the full duration of the race. The ability to keep performing and going is important in all three sports.

Muscular Endurance: In athletics is essential in the leg movements, as the athlete will be producing muscular contractions during the race, in football the player will also require muscular endurance for legs also, as the player will be running, tackling, passing and shooting. All these movements involve the muscles of the legs. In tennis however it is different, the tennis player will require muscular endurance, but in the top half of their body as well as the legs. The reason for this is that the player will need to use the muscles of the arms, shoulders and back when hitting the tennis ball; this is likely to occur many hundreds of time during the game. The tennis player will also require muscular endurance in the legs due to movement around the court.

Flexibility: A degree of flexibility is required in all three sports. However football and tennis are the sports that require the greatest degree of flexibility. The reasons for this are the footballer and tennis player need to respond to a moving stimulus. The ball and their opponents. Flexibility is required around the shoulder joint for hitting the ball, flexibility required around the hip joints when stretching for a tennis shot. In football flexibility is also required around the shoulder joints when a throw in occurs, flexibility is also needed around the hip joint when stretching for a tackle, passing and general running (as in the stride pattern). A goal keeper may also require extra high levels of flexibility, as the keeper may have to respond to a shot and tip the ball over or around the posts. In middle distance running, the athlete may need some flexibility, but not to the levels of the other two athletes, some is required around the hip for maintaining stride pattern, although the shoulder joint is needed when using the arms in sprinting, a middle distance runner will try not to use this during the race, as this will waste energy.

Speed: Is a critical factor in all sports, fast movement patterns will be required in each sport, responding to the ball in tennis or football, and sprinting to win the race. In football the player will need to able to dribble with the ball at speed, the other two sports do not need this. In middle distance running, the athlete will try and maintain high levels of speed. In football, the player will be required to carry out speed over different distances, in tennis this is the same, although the distances will be less. In tennis the duration of the speed event will be far less than a middle distance event. Rallies in tennis in extreme circumstances last over a minute. Football is similar in time to tennis, a player will only carry out small time and distance movements, this is due to the nature of the game. By carrying out time and motion analysis you can chart their movements and duration of movements for each sport.

Strength: A minimal level of strength is required for middle distance track athletics, the athlete is not needed to push against an object of an opponent. The other two sports involve contact with an external object, so a greater degree of strength is required to propel the ball. In football a higher degree of strength is also needed to shield the ball from opponents and in the tackle. However it can be argued that a certain degree of strength is needed in athletics, to enable the athlete to fight for track position. In tennis strength is only required when hitting the ball, if you observe a tennis player the arm which the player hits the ball with is bigger than the non hitting arm, i.e. the strength is in this arm.

Power: Levels of power will be dependent on the sport, in tennis, when selecting the power for the shot it is important, different levels of power are required for when selecting shots. This is the same in football, different levels of power are required when passing and shooting. In athletics power is needed, but not to the degree of the other two sports, power will be required when hurdling the barriers in the steeple chase event. In all three sports some power will be also essential for maintaining running.

Body Composition: Body composition is a vital factor to consider for performance, in all three sports excess body weight will slow the athletes down; it will require them to work harder than other athletes who carry less body weight than them and will mean they become fatigued quicker. Track athletes will tend to have ectomorphoic body composition and a small degree of mesomorph (muscles required for movement). The footballer player, will have a similar body composition, but will have a greater muscular build. The tennis player will also have mesomorph and ectomorph tendencies, as extra length in the arms and legs will allow the player to get force and power into the shot, greater height in the player, will mean the player will be able to move around the court quicker and easier than smaller players.

Agility: Is needed in all three sports, each of the athletes will need to respond to differing events that may occur during their events. Although training for agility in athletics is not a vital important aspect, an athlete will need to include some agility training methods, and this is needed because an athlete may need to respond to opponents movements in the race, i.e. positioning at the start, and ensuring they do not make contact with other athletes during the race. In football, agility is a very important aspect for performance; the footballer will be required to change direction many times during the game. In tennis, agility is also important like football, a tennis player will need to respond to a variety of shot selection from their opponent.

Balance: The need for balance is more important in football and tennis than middle distance athletics. The reason for this is that in football and tennis the athlete will be off balance numerous times. For example, a player shooting for goal on one foot (an off balance shot will result in errors), a tennis player must also maintain their centre of gravity for correct placement of their shot. In athletics balance does play a role, but not to the same degree as in the other two sports, balance is required when hurdling the hurdles and maintaining an upright body position, ensuring this will equal an upright, streamlined body position.

Co-ordination: Is vital in each sport, each of the athletes needs to ensure that they coordinate their movements for success. In tennis you need to coordinate arm movements with hitting the ball. In football coordination is required when in possession of the ball, being able to dribble is vital for successful performance. In athletics coordination is vital the athlete needs to ensure they do not make contact with other athletes. However the need for coordination is greater in football and tennis as they are coordinating movements with an external object, whereas in athletics the athlete is only coordinating running. All these factors ensure coordination is vital for all three sports.

Reaction Time: Is necessary for all sports, it is essential for athletic performance, the athlete needs to react to the gun at the start and respond to other athletes moves during the race. In football the athlete will need to respond to several stimulus throughout the game, the quicker the player can respond the quicker they can get into the correct position. In tennis, reacting quickly is also vital, they will be able to respond quicker and get into correct position. In football and tennis it is choice reaction time, in athletics, it is simple reaction time the athlete responds to one stimulus at the start, the gun going off.

Training and Fitness for Sport
Unit Number 3 Task 2

P2 Describe one method of fitness training for six different components of physical fitness

Enclosed Report

M2 Explain one method of fitness training for six different components of physical fitness

Flexibility: There are two forms of flexibility, active and passive flexibility. Both forms involve the athlete's range of motion around a joint. Active flexibility involves the full range of motion around the joint with no resistance to the movement an example of this is kicking a rugby league conversion without resistance from any of the anatomical structures around the hip, hip joint, hip flexors, hamstrings. The static flexibility is where an athlete performs a movement slowly and constant.

A method of training for flexibility includes proprioceptive neuromuscular facilitation stretch. This Hold – Relax stretch involves the athlete and a partner. To perform this method the athlete must perform a passive stretch of a muscle for 10 seconds, the athlete's partner will then applies a force to the muscle while the athlete holds and resists the movement. This stretch with the partner is held for 6 seconds. The athlete will relax and then carry out a passive stretch, the athlete should be able to go beyond the first range of motion (past the movement point in the first stretch).

Strength: is the ability to exert a force, strength can be trained using the following methodology, an athlete needs to work out their one rep maximum, this can be done by using resistance machines, once a 1 rep max has been calculated an athlete needs to work at a percentage of this figure and perform pyramid sets, of 10, 8, 6 reps, each set gets heavier, each is calculated set to a percentage of their 1 rep max.

Muscular Endurance: is the ability to perform a movement without becoming tired or to the point where exhaustion occurs where levels of performance can not occur. To train for muscular endurance an athlete must carryout both aerobic and anaerobic activities. The athlete needs to perform an exercise repeated times using the same set of muscles. If using a weight resistance machine, the athlete should concentrate on performing the exercise with a high number of reps but a low weight in comparison for training for strength.

Power: is the force of acceleration in performing movements. To train for power, the athlete needs to carry exercises that are jumping and bounding activities that combine strength and speed. An example could include jumping and bounding over mini hurdles.

Aerobic Endurance: is the ability to keep performing an exercise at high levels. To increase aerobic endurance an athlete needs to increase the distances that they train, train close to, but not exceeding their aerobic threshold.

Speed: Speed is the ability to perform a movement quickly. To train for speed an athlete needs to concentrate on distances that are appropriate for their event. A sprinter for example would concentrate on distances up to 100 m. Methods of increasing speed would be using resistance equipment, including weighted sledges, harnesses and parachutes.

Task 2
Report to the Leisure Centre
Components of Physical Fitness
Fitness Training Methods to Improve Specific Components of Fitness

This report is to aid the local leisure centres with describing methods of fitness training for the following components of physical fitness, flexibility, strength, muscular endurance, power, aerobic endurance and speed.

Flexibility: Flexibility is the ability to perform a movement over a range of movement. Flexibility can be trained by stretching the muscles.

Strength: is the force exerted by a muscle against a resistance. Strength can be trained by weight training.

Muscular Endurance: is the ability to perform a movement without becoming tired. Muscular Endurance can be trained by exercises using the same sets of muscle groups, sit ups and static contractions.

Power: is the force of acceleration in movement, a method of training for power is by carrying out gymnastic types of activities, jumping and bounding exercises.

Aerobic Endurance: is the ability of an athlete to keep on performing, a technique of training for aerobic endurance is by increasing the time and distance when exercising.

Speed: is the ability of an athlete to perform a given movement quickly, a method for training for speed is by practising techniques in the event that the athlete performs.

ASSESSOR FEEDBACK FORM

BTEC NATIONAL DIPLOMA IN SPORTS STUDIES

ASSESSMENT REPORT	**Unit:** Training and Fitness (Unit 3) Assignment 1 Fitness for Sport	Lecturer:

STUDENT NAME:	Learner 3

GENERAL COMMENTS

You have produced an assignment of very good quality. In the process you have gained all of the available assessed grading criteria - well done. You have understood and answered all tasks well showing high levels of ability and knowledge. You have successfully described P1 and explained (M1) the physical and skill-related fitness requirements of three different sporting activities. Each sport is covered well and in detail. You have also successfully described (P2) and explained (M2) one method of fitness training for the six different components of fitness. You have also shown particularly good levels of subject understanding during this task. You have successfully compared and contrasted the physical fitness requirements and skill-related fitness requirements for three sporting activities (D1). You include a table which indicates where physical and skill-related fitness occur in football, athletics and tennis which was very informative and you back this up by comparing and contrasting the three sports.

ASSESSMENT CRITERIA	ACHIEVED
P1 Describe the physical fitness requirements and skill-related fitness requirements of three different sporting activities	**YES**/NO
P2 Describe one method of fitness training for six different components of physical fitness	**YES**/NO
M1 Explain the physical fitness requirements and skill-related fitness requirements of three different sporting activities	**YES**/NO
M2 Explain one method of fitness training for six different components of physical fitness	**YES**/NO
D1 Compare and contrast the physical fitness requirements and skill-related fitness requirements of three different sporting activities	**YES**/NO

ACTION

All of the available assessed grading criteria have been awarded. In all future assignments in this unit ensure that future work is of the same level and standard. Well done again.